LUCID
DREAMING
for Beginners

About the Author

For more than twenty years, Mark McElroy designed training for MCI, Office Depot, Staples, and other major companies. Since 2002, he has written nine books on divination and has designed three decks, including *The Bright Idea Deck, The Mona Lisa Tarot,* and *The Tarot of the Elves.* He is also the editor-in-chief of the popular Tarot news and entertainment site, TheTarotChannel.com.

LUCID
DREAMING
for Beginners

Simple Techniques for Creating Interactive Dreams

MARK McELROY

Llewellyn Publications
Woodbury, Minnesota

FIRST EDITION
Fifth Printing, 2013

Book design and layout by Joanna Willis
Cover design by Adrienne Zimiga
Cover art © 2009 GoodShoot/SuperStock

Llewellyn is a registered trademark of Llewellyn Worldwide Ltd.

Library of Congress Cataloging-in-Publication Data
McElroy, Mark, 1964–
  Lucid dreaming for beginners : simple techniques for creating
    interactive dreams / Mark McElroy. — 1st ed.
      p. cm. — (For beginners)
  Includes bibliographical references.
  ISBN 13: 978-0-7387-0887-4
  1. Lucid dreams. I. Title.
  BF1099.L82M34 2007
  154.6'3—dc22

                                                          2007004831

Llewellyn Worldwide does not participate in, endorse, or have any authority or responsibility concerning private business transactions between our authors and the public.

All mail addressed to the author is forwarded but the publisher cannot, unless specifically instructed by the author, give out an address or phone number.

Any Internet references contained in this work are current at publication time, but the publisher cannot guarantee that a specific location will continue to be maintained. Please refer to the publisher's website for links to authors' websites and other sources.

Cover model used for illustrative purposes only and may not endorse or represent the book's subject.

Llewellyn Publications
A Division of Llewellyn Worldwide Ltd.
2143 Wooddale Drive
Woodbury, MN 55125-2989
www.llewellyn.com

Printed in the United States of America

For Dad,
who still visits me in dreams.

Also by Mark McElroy

The Bright Idea Deck

The DaVinci Tarot (Companion Guide)

The Tarot of the Elves

The Mona Lisa Tarot

I Ching for Beginners

Putting the Tarot to Work

Taking the Tarot to Heart

What's in the Cards for You?

The Absolute Beginner's Guide to Tarot

Contents

Preface:
In Search of the Conscious Dream

No matter how self-directed we are in life, in our dreams, most of us are hostages.

Our physical bodies paralyzed by sleep, we find ourselves in an alternative reality. The rules of the waking world—gravity, linearity, logic—may or may not apply. Identity becomes liquid. Our friends shimmer, transforming abruptly into strangers, while total strangers strike us as lifelong friends. A long-lost lover may join us at the table with our deceased mother, who happens, in the dream, to be dating Tom Cruise . . . and, in the dream, this strikes us as perfectly normal.

Not even our sense of self is sacred. Sometimes, we experience dreams in first person, seeing the dreamscape through our own eyes. At other times, we step outside ourselves, becoming both observers and participants. When we catch our own reflection in a mirror, we may even discover we have become someone (or something) else entirely.

We may find ourselves back in school, unprepared for tests and unable to remember locker combinations. We may interview for a new job, and realize, only after the interview begins, that we are completely naked. Or we recall, with sudden and thrilling clarity, that we know (that we've *always* known!) how to fly . . . and find ourselves sailing, unfettered, through the skies.

The dreamworld may be happier . . . or more threatening. Events may delight us . . . or terrify us. Our actions may be restricted by waking-world ethics . . . or we may give in to long-repressed desires. We may relive the past . . . or we may glimpse a possible future.

We spend a third of our lives asleep, and a significant portion of that time is spent in the twilight realm of dreams. Given all the time we spend dreaming, we might expect to achieve, over time, some degree of mastery over dreams.

For most people, though, this is not the case. Like an audience forced to watch a movie chosen by an unseen projectionist, the vast majority of people usually find themselves strapped in, staring at the screen, completely at the mercy of their own subconscious. They go where their dreams take them, they see what their dreams show them, and they have no choice in the matter.

This is not the situation, though, for *lucid dreamers*— those of us who, through natural ability or dedicated practice, have achieved a degree of control over our dreams. In a lucid dream, the dreamer "wakes up" —that is, becomes aware that he or she is dreaming—without literally waking up. This shift in awareness allows the dreamer to become the director, producer, and star of his or her own dream, changing the setting, the plot, and the cast of characters on a whim.

Lucid dreaming puts the infinite possibilities of the dreamscape under your conscious control. Instead of passively enduring whatever pleasures or terrors dreams bring their way, lucid dreamers do what they want to do, see what they want to see, and experience what they want to experience in a world where they are, for all practical purposes, a god or goddess.

＊ ＊ ＊ ＊ ＊

For as long as I can remember, my dreams have been remarkably vivid. As a kid, I frequently endured terrifying nightmares, the worst of which—a recurring dream—involved being attacked by a severed hand.

In these dreams, I would typically be "half-asleep, half-awake"—conscious, eyes open (or so I believed), but unable to move. This sort of "waking paralysis," I would learn later, is quite common; with practice, a lucid dreamer can turn it to his or her advantage.

At the time, though, I had no knowledge of lucid dreaming. As I lay helpless, the severed hand would approach, spider-like, from the foot of my bed. It was tangible: heavy, meaty, and hot. Its weight would shift the sheets; its progress would make the bedsprings creak.

Once positioned on my chest, it would tense, preparing to pounce. At the last minute, I would somehow shatter the spell, kicking my legs, thrashing my arms, and sending the severed hand flying across the room, where it would land on the hardwood floor with an audible *thud* before scurrying away.

Fortunately, not all my recurring dreams were like this one. Several times—always very early in the morning, when the light coming through my windows was dull and gray—I was visited by an airborne strand of friendly, brightly colored lights.

Once again, I would be rendered immobile. While I might manage to turn my head from side to side, my arms and legs would be too heavy to lift. During these dreams, though, I had the sense that the paralysis was for my own protection. Instead of feeling trapped, I felt safe.

Even so, I was not a passive observer—I was an active participant. I could think of a word, and the chain—made up of red, green, and blue points of light, each no larger than a firefly—would render that word in glowing, cursive script. I could think of a question, and the lights would form the words *Yes* or *No*. They would stream around my bedroom, amusing me with random patterns and performing aerial acrobatics at my command. Just before sunrise, they would streak out the window and disappear.

As I grew older, I stopped being visited by both the severed hand and the chain of lights ... but I also never forgot the thrill of connecting with and influencing the actions of dream visitors.

As a young teen, I became fascinated with the idea of directing the dreamscape. In an effort to control the content of my dreams, I would chant the name of my favorite actor while falling asleep.

My success rate varied. Ultimately, William Shatner—the suave captain from the original *Star Trek*, not the egotistical elder partner from *Boston Legal*—did turn up in a dream or two. To my great delight, I was even able to invite Mr. Shatner to a gospel meeting and convert him to Christianity. (In retrospect, even *I* think that sounds pretty weird and sad. But what can I say? I was a closeted geek being raised in a fundamentalist church!)

Perhaps because of that fundamentalist background, my interest in dreams and dream control eventually waned. My Bible brimmed with dreamers and their dreams—Jacob's ladder, Joseph's bowing stars and sheaves of corn, wise men warned not to repay a visit to Herod. But God, we were taught, no longer spoke through dreams; they were, today, nothing more than mental garbage, bagged up and set out nightly by the sanitation engineers of our subconscious minds.

* * * * *

I lost interest in dream control until my college years, when I came across an article on lucid dreaming in *OMNI* magazine. In it, dream researcher Stephen LaBerge provided basic information on achieving *lucidity*—a sustained, consciously controlled dream state—and tips on increasing the frequency and duration of lucid dreams. Fascinated and excited, I read the article aloud to the other three guys who shared my apartment with me.

Ray, my least imaginative and least favorite roommate ever, frowned and shook his head. "I don't get what that article is trying to say."

"People are learning to be lucid dreamers," I said. "Even while asleep, they're conscious. They decide what they want to dream about. In their dreams, they do whatever they want to do."

Ray looked genuinely confused. "But that's normal, isn't it?"

I hesitated. "I'm not sure what you mean."

Ray took a big bite of his sandwich and, as was his custom, talked with his mouth full. "What's so special about doing that? Isn't that what everybody does, anyway?"

This got my attention. "You've got control of your dreams?"

Ray nodded. "Don't you?"

Had it been anyone else, I would have dismissed the claim entirely. Given Ray's complete lack of imagination, though, I eventually came to believe his story. Ever since childhood, Ray had been a lucid dreamer. By day, he was simply Ray . . . but by night, every night, he fought monsters, bedded beauties, and flew through the air with the ease of a superhero.

In fact, to Ray, the idea that the rest of us had to work at lucid dreaming came as a visible shock. "Man," he said, "that sucks. I mean, if you can't use dreams to do whatever you want to do, why bother dreaming at all?"

Determined to beat Ray at his own game (at the time, I remember thinking that if Ray, of all people, could have lucid dreams, *anyone* could!), I once again set my sights on becoming a lucid dreamer. For a full two weeks, I followed a strict lucid dreaming regimen: every night, I spent the five minutes before bed telling myself, "I will have a lucid dream tonight!"

Nothing happened. I eventually lost interest and my lucid dreaming experiment fell by the wayside. (Hey, give me a break—I was only twenty-two!)

* * * * *

Back in 2001, as an offshoot of my work with Tarot, I began keeping a detailed dream journal. Perhaps because of my focus on recording and recalling dreams, I started coming across more and more references to lucid dreaming. While reading John Horgan's incredible book *Rational Mysticism*, I stumbled on a treasure trove of information:

- References to lucid dreaming date back at least to Aristotle.

- Even skeptical researchers have been able to teach themselves to have lucid dreams.

- Surveys indicate "seven in ten people can recall at least one lucid dream."[1]

This reading took me to the web, where I found references to a letter by St. Augustine, reprinted in Morton Kelsey's book *God, Dreams, and Revelation*.[2]

---

1 John Horgan, *Rational Mysticism* (New York: Houghton Mifflin Company, 2003), 112–13.

2 Morton T. Kelsey, appendix E in *God, Dreams, and Revelation: A Christian Interpretation of Dreams* (Minneapolis: Augsburg Fortress, 1991), 240.

In this letter, written in 415 CE, St. Augustine relates the lucid dream of Gennadius, a Roman physician, who, on consecutive nights, was met by a "youth of remarkable appearance and commanding presence." The young man prompted Gennadius to recall that he was, in fact, asleep and then went on to call attention to Gennadius's ability to see, hear, and move about in dreams exactly as he could when awake.

Lucid dreams, then, are nothing new. Still, it would be more than fifteen hundred years after St. Augustine before lucid dreams would attract the attention of serious researchers. In 1913, Frederick van Eeden, a Dutch psychiatrist, described conscious dreams and even coined the term *lucid dreaming* ... but his contemporaries, including Freud, were not particularly impressed or interested.

In the end, in-depth inquiry into lucid dreaming began with the work of Stephen LaBerge, a dream researcher at Stanford. (His work was paralleled—and confirmed—by British researcher Keith Hearne at Hull University.) LaBerge hit on the idea of using controlled rapid eye movements, or REMs, to send signals to those observing him sleep. His work (covered in more detail later in this book) provided some of the first hard evidence that some people could, in fact, remain conscious while asleep and dreaming.

Eventually, as I continued reading, curiosity got the better of me. This time around, I paired that curiosity with the tenacity I possessed at forty, but lacked at twenty. I did my research. I outlined a series of activities I hoped would inspire lucid dreams. I stuck with them, even when a month went by without results.

Sixty days later, I had my first lucid dream.

Since then, my achievements have surprised even me. In dreams, I've visited with my father, who died in 1990. I've spent time with old friends. I've inserted myself into favorite television shows and movies. I've flown, breathed underwater, and traveled in time.

I can't yet match my former college roommate's claim of 100 percent lucidity 100 percent of the time. (For reasons covered later, I'm not sure I want to.) That said, I have achieved an important insight: lucid dreaming is, in the end, a skill. As a skill, it can be learned. Once you learn it, it can be practiced and perfected over time.

If I can do it, you can, too! Apply yourself to the program outlined in this book, and soon, you, too, will join the ranks of lucid dreamers.

Mark McElroy
Winter 2005

Acknowledgments

My heartfelt thanks go out to all the members of the Comparative Tarot community and others who were willing to share their experiences with lucidity. Your stories and insights have made this book much richer.

I am also very grateful to Nanette Peterson, who waited patiently for me to reassemble this book in the months following Hurricane Katrina.

one

Introducing the Lucid Dream

In this chapter, you'll discover:

- What lucid dreams are, and what having a lucid dream is like
- How dream cues can help you recognize that you're dreaming
- How you may already have more control over dreams than you realize
- The real-world benefits of lucid dreaming

Are You Asleep?

Right now, at this very moment, are you awake ... or dreaming?

"What a silly question," you say. "I'm reading this book! Of course I'm awake!"

Okay, you're awake. For a moment, though, let's *pretend* you're asleep. Do whatever you have to do to embrace this idea. Tell yourself firmly: "I'm asleep. This is a dream. I am not reading *Lucid Dreaming for Beginners*. I am *dreaming* of reading *Lucid Dreaming for Beginners*."

Testing Your Reality

Now that we've established that you're dreaming, take a good look around.

If you're at home, look at the furniture, the knickknacks, the books, the clock on the wall. Is everything where you left it? Do any items seem out of place? Is there a long-lost toy from your childhood in the corner? Has the room changed color, size, or shape? As you strive to see this familiar place with new eyes, pretend you're being tested. One item in your room is wrong: out of context, out of time, out of place. Can you spot it?

If you're away from home, explore the setting you find yourself in. What sounds do you hear? Are all of them appropriate? Look at the people around you. Are they all strangers? Do any of them seem oddly familiar? Are they dressed as you would expect?

And what about the world around you? Do any features strike you as unusual? Do clocks and watches possess the faces, hands, or numerals you would expect? Check lettered signs: on restroom doors, above restaurants, at street corners. Read them twice. Do they say the same thing both times?

And what about the text of this book? Does the paragraph above say what it said a second ago? Look and see, just to make sure. For that matter, does the text of *this* paragraph make sense, saying what you expect it to say, or does it garrulous concept ratchet clone, a meal in gusset hammer?

Grading Your Dream Test

Think fast: when you came across the nonsense words in that last sentence—how did you feel? Was there a split second of confusion? Did you do a double take? Did you reread the nonsense, trying to make sense of it?

Did you wonder, even for a moment, whether or not you might, indeed, be dreaming? If so, congratulations: you've just taken your first step toward having your own lucid dreams.

What Is a Lucid Dream?

Lucidity: A Simple Definition

Put simply, lucid dreams are dreams in which the dreamer

a) becomes aware that he or she is dreaming, and

b) achieves a degree of control over the content and direction of the dream.

Once an experienced lucid dreamer recognizes that she's experiencing a dream, she is able to tailor the setting, the characters, and the action to suit her personal tastes.

Lucid Dream Cues

In a typical lucid dream, a dreamer notices some small detail—generally referred to as a *dream cue*—that alerts her to the fact that she's dreaming. Dream cues vary from person to person and from dream to dream, but typical dream cues include:

Unusual clock faces
- Clocks without hands
- Clock faces with unusual numbers
- Clocks with blank faces
- Clocks with faces that spin or rotate

Unstable text
- Books with unusually difficult or illegible text
- Headlines or signs with shifting or changing words
- Newspaper pages filled with nonsense text

Objects used or made in unusual ways
- A snake used as a shoestring
- An appliance that needs no power cord
- A square umbrella
- An elevator keypad without buttons or labels

Impossible actions and occurrences
- Human flight
- Shapeshifting
- One person or place suddenly being exchanged for another

- Deceased relatives restored to life
- Old friends who haven't aged

More Real Than Reality?

In my own experience—and in the experience of other lucid dreamers—lucid dreams are unusually vivid and intense. They are easier to recall than other dreams. For several minutes after waking from a lucid dream, the real world, for several minutes, may feel less "real" than the dreamworld! This confusion fades quickly, though, and is replaced by a mild euphoria that follows the dreamer throughout the day.

If you've never had a lucid dream of your own, though, the very idea of a "controlled dream" can sound bizarre ... or even frightening. With an eye toward helping you better understand the experience, here's a record of one of my own lucid dreams, experienced while researching and writing this book. It possesses many of the qualities common to lucid dreams—qualities you'll eventually come to recognize in lucid dreams of your own.

A Typical Lucid Dream

I am sitting in an unfamiliar restaurant, surrounded by a crowd of happy strangers. At a nearby table, a woman feeds her baby spoonfuls of bright-green peas. A couple near the sunlit windows holds hands and giggles softly. Waiters in white shirts, starched aprons, and dapper slacks wander the room, carrying huge trays topped with stainless steel domes.

The atmosphere is pleasant enough, but I am concerned with the menu. Instead of being printed on a sheet of paper or bound into a folder, the menu is posted to a massive electronic board (like those Arrival/Departure boards in American airports or European train stations) that runs the entire length of the restaurant. Whenever new dishes become available or the kitchen runs out of a daily special, the board updates itself. As the entries change, a deafening clatter fills the entire space, disrupting conversation and causing us all to put our hands over our ears.

Every time I try to read the board, an update occurs. Appetizers come and go, main dishes appear and disappear, and the list of desserts moves from one end of the board to the other. Casey, a friend I haven't seen since college (still in his twenties, despite the passage of two decades), walks up and hands me a printed menu. "Try this," he says, waggling his bushy eyebrows. "You'll like it better."

Looking down, I discover the entire menu is printed in a bizarre cursive font. Letters loop and curl; worse, the text has been formatted into a series of spirals, requiring the reader to spin the menu in order to read it. I struggle to make a choice, but the items themselves keep shifting: shrimp scampi becomes filet mignon becomes chicken becomes Soup of the Day.

I sigh. By the time I manage to place an order, I'll be late for work. I check my watch, and I'm surprised to see it has no hands. Instead, the entire face of the watch pivots, compass-style, each time I flex my wrist.

And then it dawns on me. *Shifting text. Friends who haven't aged. Odd timepieces.*

I'm dreaming!

The realization is almost enough to wake me. The room fills with gray fog. Features become indistinct, and sounds become hollow. People vanish.

I struggle to stay in the dream, but the harder I fight to stay in the restaurant, the faster the scene crumbles. Just in time, I remember an important technique: instead of struggling, I stand up, stretch my arms out to either side, and start to spin around in circles.

Spinning doesn't restore the restaurant—the space around me shifts unpredictably, becoming a bedroom, a mall, and an office in rapid succession—but it does plant me firmly in the dream state. Once reasonably sure I won't wake up, I stop spinning and pause to get my bearings.

The room I've landed in is a remarkable replica of the living room in my childhood home. The dining room table, the green recliner, and the bulky couch are arranged exactly as they were in the 1970s. The low coffee table is decorated with knickknacks I haven't seen in years: a wax rose in a glass sphere, a yellow candy dish, a floral vase. Even the carpet is worn in all the right places.

Tonight, though, I'm not interested in visiting my home. I take a moment to focus on my goal, then cross the room to the coat closet. To my delight, I find the door opens on a sunny meadow carpeted with soft grass—the perfect spot for a flying lesson. Even before I spread my arms, I start bobbing skyward. With each step, I rise several feet above the ground before falling gently back to earth.

A sudden flash of insight reminds me that, before flying, I have to hunch my shoulders and straighten my spine in a very specific way. Seconds later, I'm sailing effortlessly through the air, looking down at the treetops, completely free.

The Lucid Dreaming FAQ
Can I really learn to control my dreams?

While dream control may strike us, at first, as far-fetched, most of us will admit, with some reflection, that we can and do possess some (often unintentional) ability to influence certain aspects of our dreams:

- **Bringing waking stress to the dreaming world.** At work, Riccardo's team is under tremendous pressure to meet an aggressive deadline. Riccardo and other team members come in early, work all day, and stay late. At home, Riccardo collapses on the couch—and, almost every night, endures restless dreams: distorted images of his workday. He struggles to organize files and assemble his part of the report; despite his best efforts, though, the files and reports transform into meaningless chains of illegible words. The next morning, he's exhausted and angry—even when sleeping, he can't escape his stress!

- **Extending an intense experience.** After skipping television to invest four hours in focused study, Bashir relaxes and rewards himself by playing his favorite video game. Two hours later, he climbs into bed. The minute he closes his eyes, it seems, he sees the video game again. "I kept seeing the screen, the characters, the falling rocks. I'd wake up with my hands twitching, just like I was using the controller. And I would get so angry, telling myself, 'You're not playing the game any more. Just go to sleep!' But the minute I drifted off, I would see the game again. This went on all night!"

- **Processing fears through symbolic nightmares.**
Patricia, having lost a good job, is having trouble finding a new one. "I'd been interviewing for weeks, with no end in sight. People would promise callbacks that never came. When I'd check back with an interviewer who said I sounded just like what his company was looking for, he wouldn't return my calls. Meanwhile, my savings account was dwindling every day." Once in bed, Patricia began having startling dreams: intruders bursting into her bedroom. "They were coming to take the furniture," she says. "I laugh about it now, but when these dreams were going on, night after night, it was terrifying. I dreaded going to sleep, because I knew, an hour later, those men would burst into my room." Two weeks later, Patricia got a job; the dreams ended abruptly and never returned.

- **Disrupting dream cycles with late-night eating.**
Angelique had been on a strict diet for several weeks, but "fell off the wagon" for a friend's birthday. "We went out late and I had the first pizza I'd eaten in six weeks. Let's just say I had a lot of pizza, okay? When I got home, I had terrible heartburn. When I tried to go to sleep, I kept having terrible, confusing dreams:

having babies, being buried—and this really weird
one about going running with a tight, tight girdle on.
I could barely breathe. Needless to say, no more late-
night pizza for me."

- **Influencing dream content with meditation or atten-
  tive focus.** Shandra set herself a goal of reading the
  entire Bible in the course of one year. She kept the
  book beside her bed and read each day's designated
  quota of words like clockwork. Soon, she found the
  practice relaxed her and put her in a good frame of
  mind for sleeping. "And then, almost before I knew
  it, I started dreaming these Bible dreams. I would
  be in these desert places, with camels and tents and
  women carrying water pots. I would see characters
  and say to myself, 'Oh, that's just Jacob' or 'Oh, there
  goes Abraham.' The detail—the roughness of fabrics
  or the smell of cooking meat—amazed me. When I'd
  have these dreams, I'd feel very much at home. I'd
  wake up and be surprised I was back in the twenty-
  first century!"

Moving from accidental influence to conscious control may, at first, seem like a monumental task. The fact is,
though, that achieving lucidity—assuming conscious control of our dreams—is a skill that can be learned and, with
practice, honed and perfected. With little or no effort on our
part, mundane daily events can exert unintentional control
over the content of our dreams. Moving to the next level—
dream control—is simply a matter of pairing deliberate fo-

cus and practiced awareness with the dreamworld's natural tendency to reflect what most occupies our thoughts.

Is learning to lucid dream difficult?

I have found my own lucid dreams to be exciting, exhilarating, and surprisingly easy to achieve. This book, *Lucid Dreaming for Beginners*, is a lucid dreaming primer. In addition to information about lucid dreams, their history, and the research investigating them, it provides a simple, step-by-step system for engineering your own lucid dreams.

The book reflects my sincere belief (a belief supported by a growing body of scientific evidence!) that lucid dreaming is a skill. And while some people will have more of a knack for lucid dreaming than others, almost anyone should be able to use the information in this book to start having lucid dreams within ninety days or less.

How common is lucid dreaming?

In the course of writing this book, I asked many people about their experience with lucid dreams. Almost everyone I spoke with had, while dreaming, realized they were in a dream. Of those people, quite a few could recall at least one or two lucid dreams; many others reported having experienced them on and off for years.

A query to one online community produced dozens of letters from people who claimed to have lucid dreams on a regular basis. Some of these people apparently have a natural affinity for lucid dreaming; others have worked to increase the frequency and quality of their lucid dreams over time.

But for the vast majority of people, the dream state is entirely passive—they go where their dreams take them. To these people, controlling a dream—changing the setting, editing the content, creating or eliminating characters at will—sounds like something out of a bad 1980s horror movie (*Dreamscape*, anyone?).

What are the benefits of lucid dreaming?

Live your fantasies. Let's cover the most obvious benefit first. For lucid dreamers, dreamtime is playtime. The act of lucid dreaming transforms any dream into your own personal theatre of indulgence.

Visit third-century Rome. Go skydiving—without a parachute. Give yourself magic powers. Buy everything your heart desires. Meet your favorite celebrity. (Heck, *seduce* your favorite celebrity!) Interview a goddess. Change your age, your weight, your hair, your clothes . . . your gender! In a lucid dream, the only limits are those imposed by your own imagination. Who wouldn't be interested in a nightly visit to a universe where real-world consequences don't exist and the laws give way to your personal preferences?

If wish-fulfillment were the only benefit, lucid dreaming would have a lot to offer. The good news, though, is that there's a lot more to lucid dreaming than the opportunity to remake the world in your own image!

Be more confident. One of my personal favorite uses for lucid dreaming is for "rehearsals." When I know my upcoming schedule includes interviews, meetings, or workshops, I use lucid dreams to practice, in a totally realistic setting, my own comments and responses.

This practice began as an offshoot of one of my favorite meditative practices: *active daydreaming*. Active daydreaming involves visualizing an event in as much detail as possible. Before teaching a class, leading a workshop, or making a television or radio appearance, I frequently rehearse the entire event in my own mind. The practice helps me anticipate questions, revise exercises, and become more familiar with my material—all at once!

Lucid dreaming takes active daydreaming to the next step. In a lucid dream, I can immerse myself in a perfect simulation. There are no repercussions for mistakes, flubbed lines, or oversights. If I don't like the way the session is going, I wipe my mental stage clean and start all over again.

The result? By the time I experience an event in the real world, I've had lots of practice in the dreamworld. I come across as better prepared, more comfortable—and much more confident.

There's another reason lucid dreaming will increase your confidence. Once you begin to have lucid dreams, you'll join an elite minority of people who are able to influence the content of their dreamscape. Even if you keep this ability to yourself, you'll be aware that you can do something that not many other people have learned to do. Knowing you possess a rare "secret ability" can go a long way toward boosting your self-image!

Know yourself. Making an effort to have lucid dreams generally results in a greater overall awareness of your dreams.

Because dreams tend to be symbolic reflections of both our conscious and subconscious awareness, becoming more aware of your dreams makes you more aware of yourself.

Kathy, a nineteen-year-old college student, kept a dream journal as part of her effort to encourage lucid dreams. "Until I kept the dream journal, I had no idea how often my dreams included images of children and babies. At least four nights a week, I was dealing with puppies, rescuing kittens, or babysitting for newborns. At first I thought these reoccurring themes had little to do with me. While I want children later, I sure don't want to have a baby now!

"But when a friend I shared my journal with saw these entries, she connected them right away with my frustration over my artwork. I've got a real problem taking work from conception to completion. Looking the dreams over, I had to agree. Over and over again, I was nurturing newborns. In real life, I was pouring tons of time and effort into new projects . . . but never finishing any.

"That was a very important realization for me. If I hadn't been trying to have lucid dreams, I wouldn't have kept a dream journal. If I hadn't kept that dream journal, I would have missed out on one of the most important personal insights I can remember having."

In addition to recording dream symbols, the dream-journal technique (described in detail later in this book) will help you keep long-term track of the activities you consciously choose for your lucid dreams. Noticing that you repeatedly make an effort to fly in your lucid dreams might prompt you to ask important questions. Why is the idea of flight so important to you? What might your emphasis on flying suggest about your personal needs and desires? What real-world situation might be represented by your urge to take off, defy the law of gravity, and soar into the clouds?

Encourage yourself. Every lucid dream provides us with an opportunity to experience the achievement of our goals. Visualizing success—especially when that success is associated with a physical or psychological goal—can be tremendously healthy and healing.

Hoping to lose weight? In your lucid dreams, you can encourage waking weight loss by experiencing, firsthand, how a lighter, leaner body will feel. You can use the lucid dream to practice resistance to temptation, getting up from the table earlier. You can even "cheat" on your diet and enjoy all your favorite foods: dream treats look, smell, taste, and feel exactly like their real-world counterparts . . . and are completely calorie-free!

Your work toward other healthy goals can easily be supplemented by a lucid dream regimen. Using the rehearsal technique mentioned earlier, you can reduce the stress you feel during high-pressure situations. When you meet real-world exercise goals, you can reward yourself with any treat you like, without regard for your real-world budget (dream checks never bounce!) or real-world repercussions (you won't have to spend an extra hour on the treadmill to work off that extra brownie!).

Heal yourself. Haunted by ghosts from your past? Confront them—and dispel them—in a lucid dream. Do traumatic events from your earlier years interfere with your enjoyment of present-day life? In lucid dreams, you can re-create and edit these incidents, changing the outcome in a way that empowers you.

Lonesome for someone who has moved away or passed on? With practice, lucid dreams can easily become a venue for visiting those people who, for various reasons, are now "out of reach." Kevin, who has just started having lucid dreams, told me: "I use the dreams to spend time with my father. We weren't together much when I was a kid, and he died before we ever really got to know each other. When I manage to meet him in my dreams, I know the person I'm meeting isn't really him—but every time I see Dad in my dreams, I wake up feeling closer to him . . . and more at peace with myself."

Lucid dreaming can even be used to help insulate young children from the terrors lurking in their nightmares. One young mother reported: "When I was a child, I suffered from bad dreams, but quickly learned that by half-waking, I could rub my eyes and do what I called 'changing the channel' to a better dream. I shared this technique with my son. Now, when he has bad dreams, he tells me he changes the channel and orders an army of cute stuffed animals to chase his dream monsters away!"

Inspire yourself. Lucid dreams, with their flexible take on reality, are the perfect playground for exploring your own personal creativity.

Writers can use lucid dreams to try out story lines, visit with characters, and explore fantastic settings. I know artists who conduct dream experiments in painting, dance, and photography long before they try the same approach in reality.

Not an artist? Almost any project can benefit from a burst of lucid creativity. Take a project from work into a lucid dream. What insights might you gather if you worked on that project in a universe without restraints? If you're facing a challenge, you can try several different approaches before implementing the solution in the real world.

Enhance your spirituality. For many people, lucid dreams are a deeply personal, totally immersive form of meditation.

After flying countless times, meeting dozens of celebrities, and scuba diving to her heart's content, Mariam felt she should be using her occasional lucid dreams to achieve more than wish-fulfillment. "I created my own personal meditative space, with incense and sculptures and stained-glass windows. At first, I just made the place. Later, I discovered I could go there at will and spend time just ... *being*. It's extraordinarily peaceful, and I always wake up with an enormous sense of calm that follows me throughout the day."

Other lucid dreamers interested in spiritual pursuits choose to have encounters with angels, biblical personalities, or even their personal deities. After watching *The Passion of the Christ*, Sheldon was inspired to visit the scene of the crucifixion of Jesus. "Visiting biblical scenes makes my faith stronger," Sheldon said. "I feel more connected to scripture after living through the passages I read."

Frustrated that her small town lacked any access to a place where she could pursue her budding interest in alternative spirituality, Thalia held lucid dream sessions with an imaginary spiritual leader she calls Ghana. "I planned out what he would look like and how he would act, and I started focusing on bringing him into my dreams. When the student is ready, the teacher will appear ... and in a few weeks, I met Ghana for the first time. He comes across with such wisdom and compassion! I always feel like a better person after meeting with him."

Explore the beyond. At least one book, *Lucid Dreams in Thirty Days*, connects the practice of lucid dreaming with expanded psychic awareness and astral projection. The authors use lucid dreaming as a technique for inducing OBEs, or Out of Body Experiences. Their program introduces a third state of awareness, between real-world consciousness and lucid dreaming, in which they claim reality takes on "some of the flexible dimensions of a dream."

I personally have no experience with psychic or metaphysical aspects of lucid dreaming. That said, I have been contacted by at least three people who feel lucid dreaming has sharpened their intuitive abilities and psychic powers, making them more receptive to others' thoughts and enhancing their ability to achieve a trance state in meditation.

Rule your next cocktail party. When conversation lags, try asking, "So, is anyone here besides me a lucid dreamer?"

Most people are fascinated by dreams in general. The topic of lucid dreaming, while more a part of mainstream culture than ever before, remains relatively new. In my experience, when people hear about lucid dreaming—especially when they realize lucid dreaming is a skill they can practice—they always want to know more.

Once you've established interest, describe one of your own lucid dreams. Share a few of the benefits listed here. Mention two or three of the exercises that encourage lucid dreaming. (If you'll point them to this book, as well, I'll be grateful!) Instead of awkward silence, you'll find yourself engaged in a lively conversation about your very own Technicolor playground of the mind.

Aren't lucid dreams just a New Age fad?

Skeptics frequently dismiss lucid dreaming as a New Age fad. In fact, lucid dreams are anything but new. In an essay written about 2300 years ago (around 350 BCE), Aristotle described dreams in which dreamers achieve waking consciousness:

> [I]n sleep, we sometimes have thoughts other than the mere phantasms immediately before our minds.... There are cases of persons ... who believe themselves to be mentally arranging a given list of subjects.... They frequently themselves engage in something else besides the dream ... hence, it is plain that not every "phantasm" in sleep is a mere dream-image, and that the further thinking which we perform then is due to an exercise of the faculty of opinion ...
>
> ... [I]f the sleeper perceives that he is asleep and is conscious of the sleeping state ... something within him speaks ... for often, when one is asleep, there is something

in consciousness which declares that what then presents itself is but a dream.[1]

In 414 CE, St. Augustine, one of the most revered of the early Christian church fathers, described a lucid dream experienced by a friend named Gennadius:

There appeared to him, in sleep, a youth of remarkable appearance and commanding presence ... the same youth appeared to Gennadius, and asked whether he recognized him, to which [Gennadius] replied that he knew [the youth] well, without the slightest uncertainty. [The youth] then asked Gennadius where [they] had become acquainted ... whether it was in sleep, or when awake ... Gennadius answered: "In sleep." The youth then said, "You remember it well; it is true that you saw these things in sleep, but I would have you know that even now you are seeing in sleep ... [W]hile you are asleep and lying on your bed these eyes of your body are unemployed and doing nothing, and yet you have eyes with which you behold me."[2]

Author and researcher Stephen LaBerge notes that Tibetan Buddhists were practicing dream yoga—a complex set of disciplines designed to extend consciousness into the dreamworld—as early as the eighth century:

Tibetan Buddhists were practicing a form of yoga designed to maintain full waking consciousness during the dream

---

1 Aristotle, *On Dreams*, The Internet Classics Archive, http://classics .mit.edu/Aristotle/dreams.html (accessed February 22, 2007).

2 St. Augustine, Letter 159, paragraphs 3 and 4, *NewAdvent.org*, http:// www.newadvent.org/fathers/1102159.htm (accessed February 22, 2007).

state. With these dream yogis of Tibet, we find for the first time a people who possess an experientially based and unequivocal understanding of dreams as solely the mental creation of the dreamer.[3]

In 1867, the Marquis d'Hervey de Saint-Denys compiled and published five years of personal dream research in what could well be considered the first lucid dreaming manual: *Dreams and How to Guide Them*. The Marquis began by focusing on dream recall; success in remembering his dreams prompted further experimentation. He soon developed techniques for inducing dreams about specific subjects (he would associate a perfume with a person or place, then generate related dreams by scenting his pillow with a specific perfume) and for waking himself from dreams.

His work, however, was largely ignored, as the prevailing scientific thought of the day considered dreams to be little more than mental indigestion. This would be the same obstacle faced by Dutch psychiatrist Frederik van Eeden, who, in 1913, coined the term *lucid dream* to describe a type of dream in which the dreamer suddenly understands that he or she is dreaming:

> The seventh type of dreams, which I call lucid dreams, seems to me the most interesting and worthy of the most careful observation and study. ... In these lucid dreams the reintegration of the psychic functions is so complete that the sleeper remembers day-life and his own condition, reaches a state of perfect awareness, and is able to direct his

---

3 Stephen LaBerge, *Lucid Dreaming: The Power of Being Awake and Aware during Your Dreams* (New York: Ballentine Books, 1990), 23.

attention, and to attempt different acts of free volition. Yet the sleep, as I am able confidently to state, is undisturbed, deep and refreshing.[4]

His contemporaries, however—including Dr. Sigmund Freud—continued to deny that dreams could be subjected to conscious control. This denial continues today. The *Skeptic's Dictionary*, for example, cites Norman Malcom's theoretical arguments (made more than a half-century ago) as the basis for denying the reality of lucid dreams. "Skeptics don't deny that sometimes in our dreams we dream that we are aware that we are dreaming. What [we] deny is that there is a special dream state called the 'lucid state.'"[5]

In light of more recent, well-documented research—especially the work completed over the last two decades by Dr. Stephen LaBerge—this brand of outright dismissal sounds more hysterical than skeptical. LaBerge and others, connected to lab equipment that verifies their submersion in the dream state, have long been able to send prearranged signals to the waking world using coded eye movements.[6]

In the end, whatever your personal beliefs about the nature and potential of lucid dreaming, the historical record is clear: people have claimed to have lucid dreams for cen-

---

4 Frederik van Eeden, "A Study of Dreams," *Proceedings of the Society for Psychical Research* 26 (1913), http://www.lucidity.com/vanEeden .html (accessed February 2, 2006).

5 Robert Todd Carroll, *The Skeptic's Dictionary*, s.v. "lucid dreaming," http://skepdic.com/lucdream.html (accessed February 2, 2006).

6 Stephen LaBerge and Howard Rheingold, *Exploring the World of Lucid Dreaming* (New York: Ballentine Books, 1990), 24.

turies. Modern science is just beginning to study and verify the phenomenon. And while it's true that members of the metaphysical or New Age community have a great deal of interest in lucid dreaming, the concept of lucid dreaming itself predates the New Age movement by well over 2,000 years.

Is lucid dreaming for everyone?

Not everyone is as taken with the benefits of lucid dreaming as I am. In interviews conducted with volunteers from the Internet, I encountered several people who felt lucid dreaming wasn't for them. Before you launch your own lucid dreaming program, you may want to take their concerns into consideration.

Control vs. comfort. "I'm in control all day," Shannon told me. "Why would I want to be in control all night, too?"

Individuals like Shannon appreciate the freewheeling, unstructured nature of dreams. For them, the idea of lucid dreaming sounds like a lot of work. Shannon and others like her believe dreamtime is a time to rest the conscious mind. She worries that increasing the frequency of lucid dreams could have detrimental effects. "There's a reason most of us don't control our dreams," Shannon says. "In the end, I decided that lucid dreaming just wasn't for me."

Shannon's fears may well be unfounded. Even the most successful lucid dreamers rarely achieve total lucidity, so they still enjoy plenty of unstructured dreamtime. In addition, two decades of intensive study have failed to associate lucid dreaming with detrimental effects of any kind.

Still, if you share Shannon's concerns, you might want to avoid encouraging lucid dreams.

Investment of effort. Lucid dreaming is a skill, and, as with any skill, learning to lucid dream requires an investment of energy, time, and effort.

Keeping a dream journal, waking up earlier than usual, disrupting your normal sleeping habits, and conducting constant reality checks consumes a lot of time and energy. For some people, increasing the frequency of lucid dreams simply isn't worth the effort. Others hear that the program may require up to ninety days before obtaining results, and they know that a program of this duration isn't for them.

If the idea of investing time, effort, and energy in a ninety-day dream-enhancement program strikes you as an overwhelming commitment, then this approach to lucid dreaming may not be for you.

Interest in dream messages and analysis. Many people believe their dreams are an important form of communication, containing messages from God, from higher selves, from deceased friends and relatives, from the spirit world, or simply from the subconscious.

Teresa told me she prefers to allow dreams to unfold on their own, because she believes their messages, as presented, are important. "I'm interested in what my dreams have to tell me without my consciously trying to alter their content. I don't pursue lucid dreams now because I want to be attuned to those messages."

I'm someone who enjoys interpreting his own dreams, so that concern makes perfect sense to me. But once again, most lucid dreamers achieve lucidity in a relatively small percentage of their dreams. Even if you see remarkable results with this program, you will likely have many non-lucid dreams that will remain ripe for interpretation and analysis.

However, if preserving the contents of *all* your dreams is important to you for any reason, the pursuit of lucid dreaming—and the completion of this program—may not be for you.

Irregular sleep schedules. Some people have jobs with "swing shifts"—schedules that shift unpredictably from one part of the day to the other. Others travel frequently from time zone to time zone, disrupting normal sleep patterns.

The program in this book was conceived and designed with a regular sleep schedule in mind. If you know in advance that your sleep schedule will be disrupted over the next ninety days, you may want to delay your participation in the program.

Disturbed sleep or insomnia. Occasionally, everyone has some minor difficulty falling asleep. However, if you often experience sleepless nights, have difficulty falling asleep, or have trouble getting back to sleep after waking up in the middle of the night on a regular basis, this program simply isn't for you.

Disturbed sleep may be stress-related; it may also be a sign of an underlying medical condition that requires a doctor's attention. While lucid dreaming has no known detrimental effects, it's probably not wise to launch a sleep-based program until these issues are dealt with. See a doctor and establish a normal, healthy sleeping pattern before starting this program.

Psychological or emotional illness. If you're struggling with psychological or emotional issues, or if you're under therapeutic or chemical treatment for emotional illness (including clinical depression), you should not begin this program without consulting a doctor first.

Chapter 1 in a Nutshell

In a lucid dream, the dreamer becomes aware she is dreaming and assumes control of the content and direction of her dream. First, dream cues—odd events or inaccurate details that break the rules of the real world—alert the dreamer to the fact that she is dreaming. Having achieved that awareness, the dreamer can change her dream's time, place, setting, or cast of characters, remaking the dream according to her own wishes.

Most people already have more control over their dreams than they realize, and more people are lucid dreamers than you probably suspect. Having a "playground of the mind" at your constant disposal has a certain appeal, but lucid dreams offer a number of benefits with impact in the real world. Dismissed for years as a quirk of perception or just another New Age fad, the lucid dream is, in fact, a powerful tool that almost anyone with a modest amount of discipline can master.

What's Next?

With the benefits explained, objections considered, and concerns acknowledged, it's time to outline exactly how this program will help you achieve lucid dreams of your very own.

In lucid dreams, you're free from the constraints of the real world—you don't have to follow the rules. As you read *Lucid Dreaming for Beginners*, you aren't bound by the conventions that normally govern the reading of books. Think of this book as a warehouse of lucid dream resources. Instead of reading it from cover to cover, you're free to jump from chapter to chapter, finding what you need . . . whenever you need it!

If you're curious about the process of sleep—and how your own sleep habits influence your ability to have lucid dreams—you'll be intrigued by chapter 2, "To Sleep, Perchance to Dream," which includes a guided tour of the physiology of sleep and dreams.

If you're wondering how easily you'll be able to achieve lucid dreams of your own, you may want to complete the Lucid Dreaming Profile in chapter 3.

If you're curious about the research and scientific evidence backing up the reality of lucid dreaming, chapter 4, "Lucid Dreaming in the Lab," will provide you with all the information you need.

If you're eager to jump right into your own lucid dreaming regimen, you can go directly to chapter 5, where I introduce the tools and techniques you'll use to achieve your own lucid dreams.

Chapter 6, "From Awareness to Lucidity," provides a detailed look at two techniques (dream journals and reality checks) you can use to enhance your overall awareness of your dreams.

Chapter 7, "In Their Own Words," introduces you to a number of lucid dreamers, provides a firsthand look at their quest for lucidity, and offers insights, tips, and techniques based on real-life experiences.

Chapter 8 examines beneficial applications of lucid dreaming—experiments for you to try and experiences for you to explore as your command over lucidity increases.

Finally, chapter 9 offers simple, straightforward, but effective methods for analyzing and interpreting all your dreams—including your lucid ones.

With that said, at this point—as will be the case in your lucid dreams—where you go next is up to you!

two

To Sleep,
Perchance to Dream

In this chapter, you'll discover:

- How preparation for a good night's sleep begins long before bedtime
- How to enhance the quality of your own sleep
- How every good night's sleep consists of a number of sleep cycles
- Which sleep cycles are most important for lucid dreamers
- How short naps may aid you in your quest for lucid dreams
- How sleep deprivation impacts your dreams . . . and your health

The Nature of Sleep

You spend as much as one-third of your life asleep. Think about that for a moment: *one-third of your life* is spent sleeping. If you live to be seventy-two years old, you'll have spent twenty-four of those years—almost a quarter of a century—asleep! Rip Van Winkle would be proud.

Since humans spend so much time asleep, you'd think all of us would be experts on the subject. But in fact, most of us know very little about what goes on when our eyelids are closed. (Most people are, after all, unconscious when sleeping!) So what *does* happen when sleep overtakes us? Why must we spend so much valuable time slack-jawed and drooling on our pillows?

You've probably heard that the body repairs itself during sleep—and it's true. While we're zonked out, our bodies are releasing vital hormones (including growth hormones) and repairing cellular damage. You also know from personal experience that sleep resets the parts of the brain that regulate emotions and perceptions. What seemed to be a tragedy last night may, come morning, seem little more than a minor irritation. For this reason, in fact, electing to "sleep on it" before making a decision is a very wise move indeed.

When you wake up after a good night's sleep, you feel relaxed and refreshed. But when a disturbing television show, a late-night pizza, or a pending tax audit prompts a night of tossing and turning, you feel drugged, dazed, and sluggish the next day. As many college students know, you can extend your awareness and curtail your need for sleep with caffeine and drugs—but this forced wakefulness comes at a price.

As someone interested in lucid dreaming, you have a vested interest in getting plenty of sound, restful sleep. In fact, the more you know about what happens during healthy sleep, the better positioned you are to pursue lucid dreams. After all—if you don't sleep, you can't dream . . . and if you can't dream, you can't enjoy the pleasures of lucid dreaming.

A Guided Tour of a Good Night's Sleep

With an eye toward learning more about high-quality sleep, buy a ticket, step right up, and board the bus: we're going on a guided tour of the Land of Lullabies. Our stops tonight will give lucid dreaming candidates invaluable insights into

- how to slow down, unwind, and prepare for a great night of lucid dreaming,
- where we go and what we do while we're asleep, and
- what happens when we fail to get the rest we need.

Tour Stop #1: Preparing Yourself for Sleep

If you think preparing for sleep begins the moment you hop into bed, think again. Preparing yourself for sleep is a process . . . and that process begins several hours before you crawl between the sheets. Let's begin by taking a look at how the typical American prepares for sleep.

SLEEP AND THE TYPICAL AMERICAN

If you'll look to your left, you'll see Samuel. He's a typical American: overweight and overworked. He gets up at five-thirty, showers, shaves, and dashes off to a seven o'clock meeting with other members of his team. On the way to work, he stops by Starbucks for a six-dollar cup of the strongest, sweetest coffee they sell ("I call it my 'go-juice,'" he says).

The rest of the day, like most of Samuel's days, is a whirl of constant activity. Because he's always a little groggy, Samuel downs several more cups of coffee ("I'd install an intravenous line for it, if they'd let me!"). He also puts away a pack of Reese's Cups at mid-morning and a Hershey bar mid-afternoon ("Love that sugar rush!"). On really bad days, he'll sneak in an energy drink or two.

Around seven, he leaves the office and heads home. Because he's strung out on empty calories, he's ravenous by the time he eats dinner ... so he overindulges, packing down about twice the amount of food he should. He washes this down with more liquid caffeine—two tall glasses of Diet Coke.

Jittery, distracted, and worried about tomorrow's sales meeting, he spends ninety minutes watching television and pouring over declining regional sales figures. By nine, he's so wired he decides to put in thirty minutes on the treadmill ("Gotta work off this stress!"). After that, he's thirsty, so he grabs a cold beer ("A drink helps me relax!").

So far this week, he's been to bed as early as ten and as late as two. Tonight, determined to do better, he decides to turn in at eleven . . . but on his way to bed, he hears his laptop signal the arrival of incoming email. He tells himself he's going to keep the session brief ("Just five minutes!"). When he looks up at the clock, though, he discovers he's spent two hours answering email, chatting with friends on the west coast, downloading new music, and visiting his four favorite web sites.

Finally in bed, he fires up the television and watches the local news (a nonstop stream of assaults, robberies, breakins, and terrorist attacks) and CNBC's latest market updates (stocks are down). By one-thirty, he's asleep, bathed in a flickering, electronic glow.

When his alarm goes off at five-thirty, he feels as though he's barely closed his eyes. "No problem," he says, making coffee as fast as he can. "I'll catch up on my sleep this weekend."

Eight Simple Tips for Better Sleep

Samuel's bedtime routine is one of the most toxic, anti-sleep regimens known to mankind. Frankly? It's also the most popular bedtime routine in America. But life doesn't have to be this way; in fact, small changes in Samuel's routine could greatly enhance the quantity and quality of his sleep.

With an eye toward helping you fall asleep and into your dreams as quickly as possible, let's take Samuel's mistakes and convert them into tips you can use to promote healthy sleep.

1. **Avoid or limit caffeine.** Throughout the day, go easy on the coffee. And the energy drinks. And the Diet Cokes. Why? All of these are sources of a very powerful and highly addictive stimulant: caffeine. Food and beverage makers are making caffeine easier to consume than ever, going out of their way to add it to places it's never been, including chewing gum, breath mints, and even several brands of bottled water.

Many of my friends have several cups of coffee at dinner, and I know at least one that always has a Diet Coke right before bed. When I ask them whether or not the caffeine keeps them up at night, most claim they don't feel the effects of the caffeine any more. To some extent, that's true: my friends are ingesting so much caffeine, they no longer feel the effects of the substance *during their waking hours.*

Their bed partners, however, tell a different story, claiming my go-juiced friends toss, turn, mutter in their sleep, twitch, and grind their teeth all through the night. Why? The longest they ever go without caffeine is when they're asleep. During the day, their bodies accommodate a steady stream of incoming stimulant. At night, when the supply cuts off, they go into the first stages of caffeine withdrawal.

You don't have to give up caffeine entirely. Instead of choking down twenty-four ounces of Brazilian mocha, try drinking an eight-ounce cup of joe. Limit sodas and tea. (Your body's probably screaming for water, anyway.) For at least two hours before you turn in, avoid energy drinks, coffee, tea, and chocolate. Remember: the less caffeine you consume during the day, the more likely you are to enjoy the rich, deeply relaxing sleep that gives rise to a healthy dream life.

2. Eat less at night. Almost all of us, from time to time, over-indulge at dinner. We work hard, we tell ourselves, and we deserve to enjoy the fruits of our labors. Problem is, in addition to the fruits of our labors, we also feel entitled to the appetizers, cheese platters, creamy pastas, pork chops, roast beef, and chocolate cake of our labors, as well.

Huge meals, on occasion, are part of enjoying what life has to offer. A huge meal at night, though, takes a terrible toll on the quality of your sleep. In the evenings, your metabolism slows down, and heavy meals take longer to digest. Worse, when lying down (as most of us are when we get ready to sleep), you're far more prone to indigestion, especially if you sleep on your right side. That uncomfortable feeling of fullness, paired with a scorching case of heartburn, is a sure-fire formula for a night of troubled sleep.

Enhance the quality of your sleep by eating a conservative evening meal. Leave some room! If you're hungry later, you can always have a light snack—some sliced turkey, a handful of nuts, or a cup of yogurt, for example—before bed. (Sleep researchers note that having a light snack, especially composed of the foods just mentioned, can actually help you get to sleep faster.)

That said, for two hours before bed, avoid heavy, fatty snacks, along with alcohol, cigarettes, and chocolate. Because these stimulate your nervous system (even alcohol, technically a depressant, can act as a stimulant in small quantities), they interfere with your ability to fall asleep.

3. Work out as early as possible. Exercise stimulates the body, revving up your heart rate, your breathing, and your metabolism in general. That's great for burning calories, but not so great at bedtime, when your goal is to wind down and get to sleep.

Schedule your exercise sessions for the morning. You'll get more benefit from the exercise, because the resulting boost to your metabolism burns more calories all day long. You'll feel fresher, more alert, and better able to deal with the challenges of your day.

When it comes to exercise, remember: the earlier, the better. If you're just not an early riser, run your laps, cycle your bike, or hit the treadmill during your lunch hour or, at the latest, in the afternoon. With an eye toward getting the best sleep possible, avoid strenuous exercise within two hours of your scheduled bedtime.

4. Establish a bedtime routine. Routines—rituals, really— are powerful; they allow us to fall into a certain state of mind without conscious effort. A bedtime routine—even a simple one—rewards your dedication and discipline by helping you fall asleep as quickly and easily as possible.

For some, the routine involves a snack, a glass of water, and prayer. For others, fifteen minutes in front of the sink, brushing teeth and swishing mouthwash, does the trick. What you do doesn't matter ... but doing the same thing at the same time makes all the difference in the world.

Your routine tells your body, "Hey! Look at what I'm doing! It's time for bed!" If you stick to your routine, your body will comply by ramping down and chilling out—even when you're traveling.

5. Set a regular bedtime. Remember when you were a kid? Mom and Dad set and enforced a bedtime—with good reason. Kids who go to bed about the same time every night fall asleep more quickly and easily than those who don't.

But kids aren't the only ones who benefit from a bedtime—you will, too. Establishing a regular bedtime and sticking to it as much as possible is one of the easiest and most helpful changes troubled sleepers can make.

As the body learns when bedtime is, the metabolism will slow, eyelids will droop, and sleepy, drowsy thoughts will occur at about the same time every night. While the occasional late night is unavoidable (and fun!), you'll do yourself (and your dream life) a favor by hitting the hay according to a consistent schedule.

If you find your best bedtime intentions fall prey to distractions—night-owl friends, tempting television shows, the call of the computer—design a path to your bedroom that side-steps them all. An hour before bed, declare these distractions off-limits. Close your laptop, switch off the television, unplug the phone, silence your Blackberry, and get some sleep.

6. Avoid television just before bed. Bright, flickering light excites your nervous system, contributes to alertness, and makes falling asleep that much harder. Televisions, with their glowing screens, arouse us and almost certainly complicate our movement toward sleep.

Many feng shui consultants (experts in creating living spaces that promote harmony and peace) forbid television in bedrooms entirely. They express concern that the fiery energy of a television set—even when turned off! —introduces disruptive energy into a room that should be a quiet, calming space. With these concerns in mind, you might want to avoid placing a television at the foot of your bed. If you absolutely can't do without a television in the boudoir, consider placing it in a cabinet. When bedtime comes, you can close the doors to shield yourself from the television's negative energy.

If you must watch television before bed, watch dull shows. A number of people I've spoken with do report that watching television just before bed is, for them, a calming experience. In talking with these folks, though, I've noticed a pattern: most of them are watching simple, undemanding shows, such as sitcom reruns or other less-stimulating fare. If you just can't get to sleep without bowing down to the boob tube, tune in shows with the least-arousing content possible. As much as you can, avoid watching the news (which, by its nature, spotlights polarizing or disturbing stories) and commercials (which, by design, command attention).

7. Avoid computers just before bed. Computers combine the flickering screen of a television with the hypnotic, on-demand content of computer games, email, and web browsers. The resulting experience is enormously seductive; in fact, it's very common for computer users to discover that they've spent two or three times longer at the computer than they intended to.

At our own house, our bedtime routine used to include a last stop to check email. Without fail, this expanded to include browsing the web, watching video, playing video games, and listening to music. Frequently, we would spend as much as an hour caught up in online content while waiting (we claimed) for the other person to say "Enough!" and head off to bed.

After weeks of disturbed sleep—including nightmares about intruders—we finally declared computers off-limits within two hours of bedtime. The result? We fall asleep peacefully, and we don't dream about fending off falling blocks, masked gunmen, or creepy zombies at all.

8. Get seven to eight hours of sleep per night. While it's true that you can, to some extent, "catch up" on lost sleep by sleeping longer on weekends, sleep researchers and doctors agree: to maintain your best mental and physical performance, you need seven to eight hours of sleep each night.

Making a commitment to adequate sleep is increasingly difficult. Employers expect more and more of us to work after hours. Telecommuting, which was supposed to give us more time away from work, has become a sneaky way of making our work available to us twenty-four hours a day, seven days a week. In addition to juggling our professional lives, we also have to make time for children, spouses, family, and friends.

Faced with all these demands on our time, it's tempting to strike "Get a good night's sleep" off our daily To Do list. Don't do it. You'll work better, play better, love better, live better, and perform better if you make getting plenty of Vitamin ZZZZ a priority.

Tour Stop #2: Exploring the Stages of Sleep

It's hard to sleep and watch yourself sleep at the same time! With that in mind, the second stop on our Guided Tour of Sleep includes a brief virtual field trip in time and space. Our destination? Your own bedroom, the last time you had a good night's sleep.

STAGE ONE

So there you are, all tucked in, your blanket drawn up under your chin and your favorite pillow wedged between your knees. You've just turned out the lights, and you're doing that adorable little snuggly thing you always do as you settle in for the night.

Watch the rising and falling of your chest. See how slowly you're breathing? We can't tell it from here, but your heart rate has slowed down tremendously, too. These are sure signs that you've entered Stage One Sleep: that delicious, drowsy state that serves as a transition between the waking and sleeping worlds.

We have to be especially quiet now, as the slightest noise—even a whisper!—can wake you. (Oddly, if awakened now, you'd very likely say you'd never been to sleep at all.) If we're very quiet, though, you'll spend no more than ten to fifteen minutes in Stage One before slipping ever so gently into Stage Two.

STAGE TWO

Aha! Did you see that? Did you see the cute little grimace flicker across your face? Did you see your feet twitch and the muscles in your arms flex? No? Then watch more closely: you're experiencing the distinctive little muscular twitches that are part of Stage Two Sleep.

Some people call Stage Two Sleep your "baseline sleep," because, while you'll descend to deeper stages later in the night, you'll bob back up to Stage Two several times during the night—about once every ninety minutes. On and off, you'll spend about 50 percent of your total sleep time here.

Your breath is slowing down even more now, and your body temperature is beginning to fall. If we were to call your name softly or make a small noise, you might flinch, but you wouldn't be quite as likely to wake up as before. But we won't do that; instead, we'll just wait around twenty minutes or so for . . .

STAGES THREE AND FOUR

Wow. Just look at you. You're zonked out!

Stages Three and Four—what sleep researchers call "slow wave sleep"—are very similar; think of them as "deep sleep" and "*very* deep sleep." (Physiologically, they're so similar, they're often lumped together.) In both of these stages, if we were to hook you up to an EEG (an electroencephalograph, or device for measuring electrical activity in the brain), we'd see a distinctive pattern of huge, slow-moving waveforms called *delta waves*.

Delta sleep is critical. Sleep-deprived people don't get enough of it, and the impact on their personality, psychology, and physiology becomes quickly evident. Remember all that hormone-secreting and cellular healing we talked about earlier? It's going on right now, during delta sleep.

Meanwhile: ready to conduct an experiment? Let's call your name and see what happens. One ... two ... three ... *now!*

Look at that! You didn't even flinch. Even if we were to shake you, you probably wouldn't wake up right away. Right now, you're as close to being in a coma as you'll ever be without ... well, without actually being in a coma!

Let's do another experiment. Watch this: I'll take out my cell phone and give you a call.

Eventually, the ringing phone wakes you up. Groggy and disoriented, you struggle to move. With great effort, you throw a hand over the telephone receiver and pull it to your ear.

"Hello," I say. "It's just me, checking in with you. Did I call too late? Were you asleep?"

"Unnngh," you say. "Unngh hunngh."

"That's all I needed! Back to sleep now, okay?"

"Gaaahh," you say, slamming the phone down. Within seconds, you're asleep again.

Chances are, in the morning you won't remember our conversation. Most of the time, if people are awakened from Stage Three or Stage Four Sleep and allowed to drift off again, they don't remember waking up. That's how deep these sleep stages are!

Children spend much more time in Stages Three and Four than adults. If you have young kids, you know what I'm talking about. When children are in Stages Three or Four, you can sing the national anthem, play the drums, carry them from one room to another, position their arms and legs in hilarious poses, and demolish the entire house around 'em . . . and, most likely, your kids won't ever wake up.

Cycling

When you've hit Stage Four, you've gone as low as you can go. If left undisturbed for the next ninety minutes or so, you'll slowly but surely start working your way back up again: Stage Four, Stage Three, Stage Two . . .

But wait! Once you get back up to Stage Two, a very strange thing happens. Instead of winding up back at Stage One, you end up in a different sort of sleep entirely.

Stage Five: REM Sleep

Come closer to the bed—you've really got to see this to believe it.

Look at your eyes. Underneath the lids, they're rolling in their sockets and darting back and forth. Those rapid eye movements, or REMs, give this level of sleep its name, and they're the hallmark of what is, for readers of this book, the most important sleep stage of all: dream sleep.

During REM sleep, or dream sleep, almost every muscle (with the exception of your diaphragm) is paralyzed. Believe it or not, that's a good thing. Many sleep researchers believe this temporary paralysis is all that keeps you from, say, eating your pillow while dreaming about woofing down that extra-large marshmallow.

Despite the paralysis, REM sleep is the most active of all the sleep states. Your temperature increases. Your breathing gets faster. And your eyes aren't the only thing jumping around—your brainwaves are, too! If we hooked you up to an EEG right now, we'd see distinctive saw-toothed waves . . . proof positive that you're having a dream.

If you're a guy, this stage of sleep very likely gives you an erection. (When I said this in one of my dream workshops, a woman in the back whispered, "What *doesn't* give men an erection?") If you're female, you may experience vaginal contractions and other signs of sexual arousal.

About ten minutes after it begins, the first REM sleep of the night switches off. Just like that, it's over! But don't worry—you'll be back. For the rest of the night, barring any unforeseen interruptions, you'll bob up and down like a submarine diving and surfacing in the Sea of Sleep.

If we took out our stopwatches, we'd discover that each round trip—from REM down to Stage Two, Stage Three, Stage Four, and then back up to Stage Three, Stage Two, and REM again—takes about ninety minutes. In addition, each time you achieve REM sleep, you'll stick around in the dreamworld a little bit longer.

Notice how the room's getting lighter? As the sun comes up, we're entering "prime time," at least as far as lucid dreaming is concerned. Your longest period of dream sleep occurs during the last hour you're in bed. Since this particular REM session ends in consciousness (instead of dipping back down to Stage Two), you're also much more likely to remember the dreams you experience during this final burst of dream activity—unless seeing your morning face in the mirror gives you such a shock, you forget everything else!

Tour Stop #3: Getting Adequate Sleep

Americans, especially, have a problem with getting enough sleep. Surrounded by twenty-four-hour Wal-Marts, distracted by five hundred 'round-the-clock cable channels, and tied to jobs that increasingly encroach on family and personal time, we're sleeping less and less.

"Sleep in America" polls conducted over the last few years by the National Sleep Foundation consistently reveal that about half of the U.S. population isn't getting enough sleep. In 2001, two-thirds of us were getting less than the recommended eight hours of sleep. One-third were getting less than seven hours. People working the most sleep the least, with those logging sixty hours per week on the job sleeping six hours a night or less.[1]

That's particularly bad news, according to Dr. David Dinges, Ph.D. Dinges, director of the Unit for Experimental Psychology at the University of Pennsylvania School of Medicine, notes that "[p]erformance becomes unstable with sleep loss," resulting in severe memory impairment,

---

1 National Sleep Foundation, "Can't Sleep? Sleep Facts and Stats," http://www.sleepfoundation.org/hottopics/index.php?secid=9& id=34 (accessed April 20, 2006).

an inability to think quickly and clearly, and slower reaction time.[2]

As a practicing lucid dreamer, the quality of your sleep becomes very important. Sleeping well goes a long way toward increasing your ability to experience and recall vivid dreams. In addition, if you get the recommended seven to eight hours of sleep per night, you'll complete several healthy sleep cycles and maximize the time you spend in REM sleep. The more REM sleep you experience, the more dreams you have ... and the more dreams you have, the more opportunities you have for achieving lucidity.

Tour Stop #4: Taking Naps

A good night's sleep is one thing; a great nap is quite another.

Especially in the past, many sleep researchers have frowned on naps, claiming they disturb the regular sleep cycle. Increasingly, though, more and more sleep experts are singing the praises of the "power nap." In *Power Sleep: The Revolutionary Program That Prepares Your Mind for Peak Performance*, Dr. James B. Maas notes that napping, done properly, improves both mood and alertness:

> A nap should be about fifteen to thirty minutes in duration. If you nap longer than thirty minutes, your body lapses into delta, or deep sleep. Delta sleep is difficult to wake from, and if interrupted or just completed, [it] can leave you feeling

---

2 Matt Pueschel, "Sleep shown as central to overall physical health," *U. S. Medicine*, July 2004, http://www.usmedicine.com/article.cfm ?articleID=898&issueID=64 (accessed April 20, 2006).

terribly groggy. ... Be consistent and make a habit of napping every day. ... Napping only on weekends is like dieting
or exercising only on the weekends ... it doesn't work.[3]

Americans and their counterparts in the U.K. tend to
frown on naps, associating them with laziness. During my
corporate career, my coworkers frequently felt worn down
and drowsy just after lunch. Instead of embracing what their
bodies were telling them and taking a quick nap, most of
them would make themselves miserable, struggling to stay
awake.

A fifteen-minute nap would have recharged their bodies
and refreshed their minds. But in our "work until you drop"
culture, a nap would also have tagged them as slackers. Who
wants to be face down on the desk when the boss walks in?
So, instead of taking quick fifteen-minute naps, they took
twenty- to thirty-minute coffee or cigarette breaks—alternatives that are far more detrimental to both personal health
and office productivity!

Naps: A Lucid Dreamer's Best Friend

As we nap, it's not uncommon to move from Stage One
directly into REM sleep—making naps a favorite pastime
of lucid dreamers.

My own naps—and those of most people I've spoken
with—follow a typical pattern. As I drift off (a process
that takes about three minutes, if I'm sleepy already), my
thoughts begin to scatter. The conversation I'm recalling

---

3 James B. Mass, *Power Sleep: The Revolutionary Program that Prepares
Your Mind for Peak Performance* (New York: Villard, 1998), 126.

or information I've been reading scrambles itself, heading off in odd directions. Images flicker on the inside of my eyelids, and my body starts to sag.

Almost without warning, I slip into a dream state. Typically, whatever I've been working on or thinking about is carried with me—which is fine, since, in this relaxed state, I often see solutions I would otherwise overlook.

In my experience, napping dreams are rarely as stable as nighttime dreams—they shatter very easily—but they are especially well-suited for achieving lucidity. Especially if I doze off while thinking, "I would really enjoy a lucid dream right now," I'm extremely likely to have one.

A SIMPLE FORMULA FOR A GREAT NAP

If you're interested in power napping, you may want to make use of a trick my friend Terrell taught me. Terrell used to be a marine, and he learned this procedure from other servicemen who swear by it.

Before settling into your nap, pick up a pen or pencil. Hold it lightly between your thumb and forefinger, as though you're about to twirl it back and forth. Position your hand so that if you dropped the pencil, it would strike a desktop or a hard floor (instead of landing, say, in your lap or on the carpet). That done, doze off.

For the first five or ten minutes, your fingers will retain their grip on the pencil. Once your nap gets serious, though, your fingers will relax, and the pencil will fall. The resulting clatter will rouse you at just the right moment. Instead of feeling groggy, you'll feel refreshed; instead of being drowsy, you'll be wide awake.

I can personally vouch for the effectiveness of this method. And, as I also know from personal experience, you will very likely wake up from your power nap with a clear memory of a very vivid dream.

Tour Stop #5: Understanding the Dangers of Sleep Deprivation

At this point, we've covered what goes on (and goes into) high-quality sleep. We've also taken a closer look at the most under-utilized health regimen in America: the afternoon nap. But no Guided Tour of Sleep would be complete without a stop in what might be the most frightening territory we cover in this book: sleep deprivation.

Fair warning: What follows isn't pleasant. In fact, these stories, in their own way, are even more disturbing than anything Stephen King has ever cooked up. If you're reading this book just before bed, you should consider saving this passage for tomorrow. Animal lovers and very sensitive persons may want to skip this section entirely.

ANIMAL STUDIES

The most dramatic insights into the nature and importance of sleep come from studies of what happens when healthy sleep is interrupted or denied. Without proper sleep, our physical and mental state deteriorates rapidly.

An animal study first conducted in 1989 demonstrates just how vital sleep can be. Researchers connected brain activity monitors to rats, then placed the rats in a circular cage divided in half by a motorized partition. Whenever the rats dozed off, the central partition would rotate, waking the rats and depriving them of sleep.

In less than twenty days, the rats died. Before dying, despite greatly increasing their intake of food, the rats rapidly lost weight. They also developed skin lesions, suggesting a dramatic depression of their immune systems. Their heart and metabolic rates skyrocketed. Strangely, when they died, they died of hypothermia ... an outcome that seemed to surprise even the researchers, who concluded that sleep might somehow be responsible for maintaining or regulating our body's temperature.[4]

CAN INSOMNIA BE FATAL?

It's unclear exactly what these studies suggest for humans. However, research into one degenerative brain disorder suggests a prolonged lack of sleep is fatal for humans, too. Fatal insomnia is a very rare genetic disease and isn't very well understood, but at some point, the thalamus—the part of the brain regulating sleep—simply stops working. Victims initially experience difficulty falling asleep. As the thalamus shuts down, the victim becomes unable to sleep at all, descending into madness, coma, and ultimately death in a slow process that takes months to complete.[5]

---

4 A. Rechtschaffen and others, "Sleep Deprivation in the Rat," *Sleep* 25, no. 1 (February 1, 2002), 68–87.

5 Dennis Murphy, "Family Battles Fatal Insomnia," *MSNBC.com*, January 14, 2005, http://www.msnbc.msn.com/id/6822468/?GT1=6190 (accessed July 2, 2005).

The Permanent Impact of Temporary Sleep Deprivation

Introducing Peter Tripp. Even short-term sleep deprivation may have tragic long-term effects, as suggested by the strange, sad story of Peter Tripp.[6] Today, most people do not recognize Peter Tripp's name, but in 1959, he was the most popular disc jockey in New York City. In addition to coming up with the idea of "Top 40" record charts, he was one of the first in the radio industry to realize the potential of television to boost interest in pop music. In short: he was a trend-setting visionary with huge popular appeal.

At thirty-two, Tripp was the proverbial picture of health. As a child, though, he had spent more than twelve months on crutches after a painful surgery to correct congenital defects in the bones of his hip. This experience likely gave rise to his desire to do something to support the March of Dimes, which, in 1959, had recently expanded its outreach to children with exactly these kinds of defects.

Peter Tripp's big idea. Ultimately, Tripp hit on the idea of raising money for charity by setting a world record. Always fascinated with sleep deprivation stories, Tripp decided to go two hundred hours (more than eight days) without sleep. To

---

6 My summary of Peter Tripp's strange odyssey into sleep deprivation is derived from a number of sources, including Dr. Stanley Coren's excellent article in *Psychiatric Times* (http://www.psychiatrictimes.com/p980301b.html), an entry at HistoryOfRock.com (http://www.history-of-rock.com/peter_tripp.htm), and the photos and summary on ManFromMars.com (http://www.manfrommars.com/tripp.html), among others.

give the publicity stunt the flavor of a scientific experiment, he enlisted two doctors—Dr. Louis West and Dr. Floyd Cornelison—to monitor his progress.

At this point, not a great deal was known about the long-term side effects of severe sleep deprivation. Dr. West had some experience treating former prisoners of war who had been tortured with sleep deprivation techniques; these men frequently claimed they no longer "felt like themselves" and suffered from permanent changes in their personalities. Though West strongly advised Tripp against doing so, the disc jockey forged ahead with his plans, and on January 20, 1959, Peter Tripp's voyage into sleeplessness began.

The challenge begins. The rules of the contest were simple: for two hundred hours, Peter Tripp would not sleep. To eliminate the possibility of Tripp sneaking in some shut-eye, aides watched him constantly—even in the bathroom. Photos were taken once an hour to document his wakefulness. In addition to monitoring his vital signs, doctors would monitor Tripp's brain activity with an electroencephalogram, or EEG.

Once the experiment began, Tripp, full of energy and bubbling with enthusiasm, delivered his broadcasts from a special studio in the heart of Times Square: the Armed Forces Recruiting Station. For the first two days, things went very well. Staying awake took little or no apparent effort, and Tripp looked well-positioned for success.

First signs of trouble. By the third day, Tripp began to feel an almost overwhelming sense of fatigue. His trademark cheerfulness gave way to a state of constant irritation, and Tripp became rude, abusive, and confrontational. At one point, he became so aggressive and insulting that a barber, hired to give Tripp a daily in-studio shave, burst into tears and refused to enter the studio again.

Rapid deterioration. Eventually, Tripp—like the rats in the experiment described earlier—began to suffer from extreme hypothermia. Shivering, he constantly wore a coat and hat—even indoors. By the fourth day, Tripp began to suffer bizarre hallucinations, seeing kittens, mice, cobwebs, and huge spiders; by the fifth day, he claimed he no longer knew whether he was the real Peter Tripp or an impostor. At one point, a vision of an approaching undertaker sent him screaming from the studio and into Times Square traffic.

Tripp became dangerously paranoid, accusing studio electricians of placing electrodes in his shoes, asserting that associates were drugging his food, and ultimately accusing his doctors of extending the experiment beyond the agreed-upon two hundred hours. Doctors monitoring Tripp noticed his worst hallucinations and breaks with reality came at predictable ninety-minute intervals—almost exactly the time it takes a sleeping individual to cycle from REM sleep to delta sleep and back into REM sleep again.

Asleep while awake. The strangest finding of all came at the end of the experiment. After two hundred hours of wakefulness, Peter Tripp's brain activity had been radically altered. His eyes were open. He walked and talked. But EEG readings confirmed that Peter Tripp, though apparently awake, was for all practical purposes asleep and dreaming. In photos from the February 9, 1959 *LIFE Magazine* feature story, Tripp looks very much like the walking dead.[7]

The aftermath. With the experiment concluded, Tripp slept for thirteen continuous hours. (Some reports claim twenty-four.) EEG records show he spent almost all of this time in REM sleep. Upon waking, he requested the morning paper and, for all practical purposes, appeared to have returned to his normal, buoyant self. *TIME Magazine* reported, "Tripp seemed outwardly well."[8]

Events in the near future, however, would suggest otherwise. Over the next several months, Tripp's personality became darker and more confrontational. His marriage ended in divorce. The former trendsetter soon lost his position with WMGM, working several short stints at other stations before leaving radio altogether and working as a traveling salesman.

Tripp's experience suggests that healthy sleep plays an integral role in maintaining physical, emotional, and psychological stability. It also suggests that a prolonged lack of sleep may have consequences—including altered mood and personality disorders—that we don't yet completely understand.

---

7 "Sleepless in Gotham," *TIME.com*, February 9, 1959, http://www
  .time.com/time/magazine/article/0,9171,892201,00.html (accessed
  July 14, 2005).

8 Ibid.

Good Reasons to Avoid Sleep Deprivation

Tripp's case is extreme, and few of us are likely to try to repeat his attempt to break a world record for sleeplessness. That said, far too many Americans consistently fail to get adequate amounts of healthy sleep. Convinced there simply aren't enough hours in the day to get things done, we respond by trimming hours off our time in bed. In doing so, we may be accomplishing by degrees just as much damage as Peter Tripp endured during his self-imposed "wake-a-thon."

One recent study by the Boston University School of Medicine established an odd link between sleep deprivation and the onset of adult diabetes.[9] Participants who reported sleeping less than five hours a night were found to be two and a half times more likely to acquire type 2 diabetes than their better-rested peers.

Losing just two hours of sleep nightly—reducing your sleep time from seven hours to five—can dramatically impair your ability to think clearly and act responsibly. A study summarized for WebMD.com found that, within just one week, people who lost two hours of sleep per night were, by Friday, just as debilitated as people who stayed awake for forty-eight hours straight.[10]

---

9 "Dire Risk if You Sleep Less than Six Hours," *CNN.com,* n.d., http://cnn.netscape.cnn.com/news/package.jsp?name=fte/ sleepdiabetes/sleepdiabetes (accessed February 2, 2006).

10 Sid Kirchheimer, "Sleep Deprivation Hinders Thinking, Memory," *WebMD.com,* March 14, 2003, http://my.webmd.com/content/ article/62/71591.htm (accessed February 2, 2006).

Sleep deprivation has been linked to weight gain, suppression of the immune system, and a host of other illnesses. As the studies just mentioned seem to suggest, cutting back on sleep for just an hour or two per night can have dramatic consequences.

Sleep Deprivation and Lucid Dreaming

One common concern expressed by people who are considering pursuing lucid dreams is the impact their efforts will have on the quality of their sleep. Understanding the importance of a good night's rest, some worry that making a conscious effort to control their dreams may keep them awake, contributing to sleep deprivation.

In light of this concern, it's helpful to keep the following points in mind:

- **Over the past several years, lucid dreaming has been very closely studied.** At no time has any research suggested that lucid dreaming is dangerous or detrimental in any way.

- **The first night I started my lucid dreaming regimen, I did have some difficulty falling asleep.** Part of this was excitement. Part of my trouble, though, was also related to trying too hard to induce a lucid dream. You can't have lucid dreams by force! The moment I quit investing so much energy in success, my sleep pattern returned to normal. Soon after, I had my first lucid dream.

- **The lucid dreaming techniques presented in this book have a great deal in common with relaxation**

exercises. Giving these exercises a try shouldn't stress you out. (If they do, you're doing something wrong!) In my personal experience, the mental disciplines, meditative techniques, and other processes involved in achieving lucid dreams actually help me fall asleep faster—and sleep better!

- **If your efforts to achieve a lucid dream consistently disrupt the quality of your sleep, you can discontinue them at any time.** Your exploration of lucid dreaming isn't compulsory. If you don't enjoy the experience, you can always crawl under the covers, close your eyes, and go back to traditional sleep and dreams.

- **If you're someone who feels there "just aren't enough hours in the day" to get things done, you're going to love lucid dreaming.** Because lucid dreaming extends consciousness into the sleeping state, you can get more things done—brainstorming, exploring your art, inventing dance moves, solving problems, overcoming obstacles—by getting *more* sleep!

Embracing Sleep

And with that observation, our guided tour of a good night's sleep comes to an end.

Like most people, you may be someone who has always taken sleep for granted—it's just what happens when you close your eyes! At this point, though, I hope our tour drove home these important points:

- **Your daily routine greatly influences the quality of your sleep.** To get the most refreshing sleep possible, eat less in the evenings, avoid stimulants, and spend the hour just before bed engaged in a quiet, relaxing activity.

- **Sleep happens in cycles.** After a few minutes in shallow Stage One sleep, healthy sleepers descend down to delta sleep (Stage Four), rise back up to Stage Two, and then slip into a unique, dream-producing sleep state called REM sleep. After this, undisturbed sleepers cycle from REM sleep down to Stage Four, and back, taking about ninety minutes to complete each trip. For lucid dreamers, REM time is playtime—an opportunity to visit a world that conforms to our every whim.

- **Short naps, in addition to improving performance and concentration, are prime time for lucid dreaming.** When we nap, we slip easily from Stage One into REM sleep. To avoid grogginess, limit your naps to no more than thirty minutes.

- **Sleep deprivation may be the most underrated health threat in America today.** Boost your performance, safeguard your health, stabilize your emotions, and sharpen your mind by getting between seven and eight hours of sleep each night. In addition to warding off physical and psychological diseases, this routine maximizes the time you spend in REM sleep, providing you with more opportunities to achieve lucidity.

Chapter 2 in a Nutshell

For anyone interested in dreams, getting plenty of sound, healthy sleep is critical. Preparation for a good night's sleep begins long before bedtime.

In the course of the night, you'll cycle through several distinct levels of sleep. For lucid dreamers, the most important of these is REM sleep—the phase of sleep in which all dreams occur. By getting a healthy amount of sleep and taking short naps, you can extend the length of time you spend in a dreaming state and give yourself more opportunities for lucid dreaming. Cut your sleep short, however, and you create a sleep deficit that works against your health just as much as it defies your lucid dreaming goals.

What's Next?

While you may freely jump from chapter to chapter, I recommend you consider reading one of the following chapters next:

In chapter 3, you'll find a lucidity profile—a short, simple test that will help you determine the ease with which you'll achieve lucid dreams of your own.

Running into skeptics who doubt the reality and power of lucid dreams? Read chapter 4, an overview of the science behind them.

Ready to start your own lucid dreaming program? Jump directly to chapter 5.

three

Your Lucid Dreaming Profile

In this chapter, you'll discover:

- The Lucid Dreaming Profile, a simple tool you can use to estimate your lucid dreaming potential
- How your own habits influence the quality of your sleep and the nature of your dreams
- Small changes you can make in your routine to encourage healthier sleep and increase the likelihood of having lucid dreams

Lucid Dreaming . . . Gift or Skill?

Presumably, if you're reading this book, you want to

a) have lucid dreams, or

b) increase the frequency and quality of your lucid dreams.

The most prominent lucid dream researchers affirm again and again that lucid dreaming is a skill. My own experience with lucid dreams and my conversations with dozens of other lucid dreamers tell me they're right: with a little discipline, dedication, and practice, almost anyone can have a lucid dream.

The question under examination in this chapter, then, is not *whether* you can assume control of your dreams, but how much effort will be required in order for you to do so. How easily will you achieve lucidity? How long will it take you to have your first lucid dream? And, once you start having lucid dreams, how easy will it be for you to have them more often?

What to Expect from the Lucid Dreaming Profile

With questions like these in mind, I designed the Lucid Dreaming Profile (LDP). The questions will explore your current sleeping habits, the factors that influence the quality of your sleep, your previous experience with lucid dreams, your ability to recall your non-lucid dreams, and your dedication to achieving lucid dreams of your own.

The LDP isn't intended to be a scientific tool, so don't expect it to generate results like, "Because your score is a 89.5, you can expect to have your first lucid dream at precisely 3:45 a.m. on November 4th." Instead, the profile is a fun, engaging way to "guesstimate" your personal potential for lucidity.

At the end of the profile, I review the logic behind each question. To make this exercise as effective as possible, you should fill out the profile completely before you read that section. (No fair peeking!) If your score isn't as high as you had hoped, this information will offer insights you can use to boost your potential and increase the likelihood of a lucid dream.

The Lucid Dreaming Profile

Answer each of the following questions honestly; at the end, a scoring guide will help you evaluate the results.

1. On average, how many hours of sleep do you get per night?
   a) Eight hours or more
   b) Between seven and eight hours
   c) Six to seven hours
   d) Five to six hours
   e) Less than five hours

2. On average, how many caffeinated drinks (cups of coffee, cans of cola, energy drinks) do you consume per day?
   a) None
   b) One to three
   c) Three to five
   d) Five to seven
   e) Seven or more

3. When do you tend to schedule your physical exercise?
    a) Early morning
    b) Mid-morning
    c) Lunch hour
    d) Mid-afternoon
    e) Evening
    Note: if you don't exercise regularly at all, choose
        answer E.

4. How often do you consume a heavy dinner meal?
    a) Never
    b) Very rarely
    c) Occasionally
    d) Often
    e) Very often

5. How frequently do you watch television just before
    bed?
    a) Very rarely or never
    b) Rarely
    c) Occasionally
    d) Frequently
    e) Very frequently

6. How frequently do you remember your dreams?
    a) Very frequently
    b) Frequently
    c) Occasionally
    d) Rarely
    e) Very rarely or never

7. On average, how many dreams or dream fragments do you remember per night?

   a) Five or more
   b) Three or four
   (c) Two
   d) One
   e) None

8. How frequently have you had lucid dreams in the past?

   a) Very frequently
   b) Frequently
   c) Occasionally
   (d) Rarely
   e) Very rarely or never

9. How frequently have you had lucid dreams in the past year?

   a) Very frequently
   b) Frequently
   c) Occasionally
   (d) Rarely
   e) Very rarely or never

10. If increasing the frequency of your lucid dreams required you to set an alarm and wake yourself up one hour earlier than usual, how willing would you be to do this on a regular basis?

    (a) Very frequently
    b) Frequently
    c) Occasionally

d) Rarely

e) Very rarely or never

11. If increasing the frequency of your lucid dreams required you to keep a dream journal—a written account of every dream you recall—for sixty days, how willing would you be to do this on a regular basis?

a) Very frequently

b) Frequently

c) Occasionally

d) Rarely

e) Very rarely or never

12. In the past, how often have you used affirmations—short, positive statements, usually said aloud, that remind you of your goals—as part of an effort to make a change in your life?

a) Very frequently

b) Frequently

c) Occasionally

d) Rarely

e) Very rarely or never

13. How often do you currently take naps?

a) Very frequently

b) Frequently

c) Occasionally

d) Rarely

e) Very rarely or never

14. How often are you involved in programs or plans that require consistent work over a period of thirty days or more to complete?

   a) Very frequently

   b) Frequently

   c) Occasionally

   d) Rarely

   e) Very rarely or never

15. When you set long-term goals, how often do you achieve them?

   a) Very frequently

   b) Frequently

   c) Occasionally

   d) Rarely

   e) Very rarely or never

16. How important is it for you to have a lucid dream?

   a) Very important

   b) Important

   c) Somewhat important

   d) Not very important

   e) Not important at all

17. How vivid do your non-lucid dreams tend to be?

   a) Very vivid

   b) Vivid

   c) Somewhat vivid

   d) Not very vivid

   e) Not vivid at all

18. How frequently do you use visualizations—vivid, detailed imaginary pictures of something you desire—as a way of encouraging you to achieve your goals?

    a) Very frequently
    b) Frequently
    c) Occasionally
    d) Rarely
    e) Very rarely or never

19. How frequently do impossible or unusual things (flight, sudden transformations, etc.) happen in your non-lucid dreams?

    a) Very frequently
    b) Frequently
    c) Occasionally
    d) Rarely
    e) Very rarely or never

20. How often has the appearance of an odd or "out of place" person, place, or thing alerted you to the fact that you were dreaming?

    a) Very frequently
    b) Frequently
    c) Occasionally
    d) Rarely
    e) Very rarely or never

Evaluating Your LDP

Scoring the profile is quick and easy! Review your responses, using the following table to calculate your final score:

- For every A, give yourself five points.

- For every B, give yourself four points.

- For every C, give yourself three points.

- For every D, give yourself two points.

- For every E, give yourself one point.

Tally your final score. In general, the closer your score is to 100, the easier it will be for you to begin having your own lucid dreams.

- **If you scored between 81 and 100,** you're likely to have lucid dreams with ease.

- **If you scored between 61 and 80,** you're still very likely to have lucid dreams, though some small life-style changes may help you achieve them more easily.

- **If you scored between 41 and 60,** you may have to invest more time and be a little more dedicated than others with higher scores, but lucid dreaming is still a distinct possibility, especially if you're willing to make changes in your lifestyle and routine.

- **If you scored between 21 and 40,** you can expect lucid dreaming to be a challenge. With discipline, dedication, and substantial lifestyle changes, you can learn to have lucid dreams, but the process may take time.

- **If you scored between 1 and 20,** learning to have
  a lucid dream will likely prove very challenging.
  If lucid dreaming is important to you, you might
  consider beginning your program by learning some
  simple relaxation techniques, cutting back on caffeine, and getting more sleep for thirty days. If these
  changes aren't practical for you at this point, you
  may not be well-positioned to pursue lucid dreaming
  at this time.

Boosting Your Lucid Dreaming Potential

If your profile score wasn't as high as you'd hoped . . . don't
despair! This question-by-question exploration of the Lucid Dreaming Profile reveals the logic behind the scoring
and includes tips for boosting your score.

To get the most out of this information,

- review your answers,
- identify any questions you answered with a C, D, or
  E, and
- check the insights associated with those questions for
  tips on increasing your lucid dreaming potential.

1. On average, how many hours of sleep do you get per night?

As mentioned during our guided tour of sleep, getting plenty
of rest is one of the best investments potential lucid dreamers can make. Getting seven to eight hours of sleep per night
relaxes the body, restores mental clarity, and encourages the
development of a stable, consistent sleep cycle.

More sleep time equals more dreamtime! If having lucid dreams is important to you, getting a healthy amount of sleep is critical. Set a bedtime and stick to it as often as possible. Getting up at about the same time every day—even on weekends—can help, too.

If you answered D or E to this question, you're not just working against your ability to have lucid dreams . . . you're taking serious risks with your health. A good long look at your priorities is overdue.

2. On average, how many caffeinated drinks (cups of coffee, cans of cola, energy drinks) do you consume per day?

Caffeine and other stimulants are the archenemies of restful sleep. (Remember: even alcohol, a depressant, acts as a stimulant in small amounts.) Especially if you claim you no longer feel the effects of caffeine or alcohol, your sleep is very likely being disrupted by overnight withdrawal symptoms—every night.

And caffeine isn't the only culprit at work here! Chocolate, while healthy in small amounts, is laced with caffeine and sugar. If you sweeten your coffee and tea with sugar, drink sweet alcoholic drinks, or guzzle canned soda and energy drinks, you're also giving yourself a sugar buzz. All of these substances have the potential to compromise the quality and soundness of your sleep. (In other words: people interested in having lucid dreams may have to forego their current bedtime habit of washing down a few chocolate-covered toasted coffee beans with an ice-cold can of Red Bull.)

If lucid dreaming is important to you, consider cutting back on stimulants and sugars. If possible, eliminate them entirely within two to four hours of your regular bedtime. If you normally have tea or soda with dinner, switch to ice water. If you are used to a cup of nightly coffee, try switching to decaffeinated green tea. You'll be healthier ... and you'll sleep better.

If you answered D or E to this question, it's likely your body is starved for good, old-fashioned water. In addition to helping you meet your lucid dreaming goals, making the switch to water can work wonders for your weight and health.

3. When do you tend to schedule your physical exercise?

Regular exercise helps maintain a sound mind and body—but you didn't need this book to tell you that, did you?

Just twenty minutes of exercise can boost metabolism for hours afterward. For those who exercise early in the day, that's great! A morning jog, a pre-office stop at the gym, or even a brisk, mid-morning walk can prime your body to burn more calories for the rest of the day. The earlier you exercise, the better.

Exercising in the evening is probably better than not exercising at all. That said, strenuous late-night exercise also boosts your metabolism for several hours, which can complicate the process of winding down and falling asleep. In saying this, I'm not recommending that you become a total couch potato. Instead, especially if lucid dreaming is important to you, I'm suggesting you might try scheduling your workouts earlier in the day.

If you're one of those folks who answered E because you don't exercise regularly at all, you're in good company. Many, many people are so caught up in work and routine that they exercise very little, if at all. If you're one of these people, you already know this works against you from a health standpoint, predisposing you to heart attack, high blood pressure, and diabetes.

It also, however, works against your lucid dreaming goals, as people who are overweight and under-exercised are far more likely to suffer from sleep apnea (a dangerous suspension of breathing during sleep) and other sleep-related disorders. A little exercise—even a brisk fifteen-minute walk, four times a week—can go a long way toward improving the quality and restfulness of your sleep.

4. How often do you consume a heavy dinner meal?

I live in the southern United States, where big dinners— fried chicken, mashed potatoes, macaroni and cheese, slabs of roast beef or steak, and brick-sized wedges of chocolate cake—are standard fare.

But you don't have to be a Southerner to find yourself packing down a huge nighttime meal. If you eat out often (and more and more of us do), you're likely to find yourself attending an inordinate number of buffets and sitting down to huge platters of oversized restaurant portions.

Wolfing down a huge dinner may make you feel sluggish and drowsy—and, at first, that may sound like a good thing for people interested in sleep and dreams. Problem is, all that food has to be digested ... and, if you're eating your biggest meal at night, it has to be digested during your sleep. While you should be enjoying your lucid dreams, your stomach is contracting and your esophagus is fighting off a severe case of indigestion.

A big breakfast is a great thing. A big lunch may make you drowsy at work. But either of these, from a lucid dreaming standpoint, is better than a heavy dinner. As often as possible, eat light at night.

And again, those of you who answered this question with a D or E, in addition to changing your habits with an eye toward lucid dreaming, should consider making some changes for health reasons, to boot.

5. How frequently do you watch television just before bed?

Depending on what you watch, television just before bedtime may not be a good idea.

Me? I'd be happier with no television in the bedroom at all. I find the flickering light of the LCD screen (or, if you're retro, the cathode-ray tube) far too energetic for a room dedicated to romance, sleep, and dreams. Even when the television is off, that little red "ready" light annoys me.

My partner, though, is all about bedtime television; he claims watching something mindless—syndicated reruns of *Malcom in the Middle* or *Dharma & Greg*, for example—helps him relax, unwind, and forget about the demands of his day. (Even he admits, though, that watching the nightly news or politically charged programming like *The Daily Show* makes falling asleep much harder.)

My advice? If lucid dreams are important to you, consider switching off the television about an hour before bed. Spend that last hour engaged in a calming bedtime routine: choosing clothes for the next day, washing up, reading a peaceful book, meditating on Scripture, or affirming your dedication to lucid dreaming.

If you answered D or E to this question, it's time to realize your television habits, in addition to working against your lucid dreaming goals, could be problematic from a romantic standpoint, as well!

6. How frequently do you remember your dreams?

Dream recall is tricky business. Dreams fade quickly; within an hour of waking, the most vivid dreams may be completely forgotten. Before I started keeping a dream journal, I would frequently recall vivid dreams early in the morning; by afternoon, though, the details of my dreams would slip away. I could remember having had a dream. I might even remember that the dream was interesting or important. But the dream itself? Gone.

Most people interested in lucid dreaming are already deeply involved in their dreams. If you're curious about your dreams, you'll quite naturally tend to remember them more often than someone who dismisses dreams as unimportant or irrelevant.

If you answered this question D or E, take heart! Dream recall improves with time and practice. Consider adding a "dream chat" to your morning routine, exchanging dreams with a friend, spouse, partner, or family member. In addition, writing down your dreams in a notebook or journal will greatly boost your ability to remember your dreams. Reading back over your dream journal entries can prove interesting, too. In the process, I frequently find myself saying, "Wow! I had forgotten about that dream completely!"

7. On average, how many dreams or dream fragments do you remember per night?

The more dreams you have per night, the more opportunities you have to "wake up" in your dreamworld, achieve conscious control, and experience lucidity.

In preparing for this book, I noticed a trend among people I interviewed: those who reported dreaming more often reported achieving lucidity more easily. If you recall a high number of dreams or dream fragments per night, my experience suggests you'll have an easier time learning to have lucid dreams.

If you answered this question C, D, or E, there are many things you can do to improve your dream recall and boost your lucid dreaming potential. Because you're usually in a REM sleep cycle just before waking for the day, setting an alarm clock to go off twenty or thirty minutes before your usual waking time works very well.

If you're able to go back to sleep easily, some dream researchers report great success with this method: they set an alarm for two hours before their scheduled waking time, stay awake for a half-hour or so, and return to bed. They report that their final ninety minutes are filled with vivid dreams.

Finally, naps also provide you with a great opportunity to boost your number of dreams per day. Set an alarm (or try the pencil trick mentioned in chapter 2), doze off, and you'll be surprised how often you bring a dream or dream fragment back with you.

8. How frequently have you had lucid dreams in the past?
9. How frequently have you had lucid dreams in the past year?

Questions eight and nine both address the frequency of your lucid dreams, so we'll cover them together.

As mentioned earlier, lucid dreaming is a skill. As a skill, it can be learned and improved with practice. That said, just as some people have a gift for music or sports, some people have a natural affinity for lucidity. The interviews I conducted before writing this book support my conclusion that people who answer A or B on these questions will have a very easy time consciously boosting the frequency of their lucid dreams.

If you answered these questions D or E, don't worry. Several people I interviewed had never had lucid dreams before trying to have them. Once they dedicated themselves to the process, they enjoyed great success.

When I started trying to have lucid dreams, lucidity was a very rare experience for me (apart from the childhood memories described earlier). Now, I have them with increasing regularity. As a general rule, I've found the following to be true:

- If you can't remember ever having a lucid dream, you'll very likely take about ninety days to start achieving lucidity with the program outlined in this book.
- If you remember the occasional lucid dream, you'll see results within sixty days.
- If you have lucid dreams frequently and are hoping to increase their frequency, you will see results in thirty days or less.

In a way, lucid dreaming is like exercise. Once you start a regular program of exercise, your strength increases slowly over time. If you've never exercised at all, even a modest work-out routine will be difficult at first. If you're in pretty good shape when you start, adopting and maintaining your exercise program will be much easier.

10. If increasing the frequency of your lucid dreams required you to set an alarm and wake yourself up one hour earlier than usual, how willing would you be to do this on a regular basis?

11. If increasing the frequency of your lucid dreams required you to keep a dream journal—a written account of every dream you recall—for sixty days, how willing would you be to do this on a regular basis?

These two questions are both related to dream-enhancement methods discussed later in this book. If you wake yourself a little earlier than normal, you'll very likely interrupt a REM sleep cycle and, as a result, remember a dream. If you write those dreams down in a notebook or journal, your ability to recall your dreams will improve over time.

Questions 10 and 11 are really asking the same thing: how dedicated are you to the idea of exploring or increasing your lucid dreaming abilities? Doing so may require you to alter some habits or acquire new ones. Are you willing to experiment with waking times? Are you willing to adopt a long-term discipline of recording your dreams? If you answered D or E, you may be resistant to making changes that, in the long run, could facilitate your quest for lucidity.

12. In the past, how often have you used affirmations—short, positive statements, usually said aloud, that remind you of your goals—as part of an effort to make a change in your life?

Affirmations have been so overused and abused by feel-good self-improvement gurus that many people now resist adopting them. Even so, affirmations—used wisely—can be very powerful tools for change. Whether you're trying to lose weight or improve a poor self-image, affirmations are a proven technique for enhancing success. They bring your goals in front of you on a daily basis and serve as reminders of your ultimate goal.

Later in this book, you'll find affirmations you can use to encourage the onset of lucid dreaming and make yourself more aware of the dream state. Unlike affirmations designed to assure you that you possess some trait or ability, these affirmations are designed to create subtle shifts in your awareness.

If you are willing to use affirmations, you will achieve lucid dreams faster than those who do not practice them. If you've used affirmations to alter behavior or emphasize goals in the past, the affirmations in this book will very likely enhance your success with lucid dreaming.

13. How often do you currently take naps?

As mentioned in the previous chapter on sleep, short naps lend themselves to the production of lucid dreams. If you're willing to add a fifteen- to twenty-minute nap to your routine, you'll increase your chances of having a lucid dream (and you'll get all the benefits of a quick nap, as well!).

14. How often are you involved in programs or plans that require consistent work over a period of thirty days or more to complete?

Though some people I've interviewed have told me they had lucid dreams within days of pursuing them, the vast majority reported that weeks or months of dedication and discipline were required before they achieved lucidity.

This was certainly the case for me. Once I decided to make having lucid dreams a goal, I adopted the journaling technique, affirmations, and visualizations as a means of encouraging them. I'm generally a fast learner, so I expected lucid dreams to begin almost immediately. Thirty days later? No lucid dreams.

At that point, I almost abandoned the program ... but stuck with it anyway, mostly because my work with the dream journal was producing a number of personal insights and positive benefits. One month later, I wavered again; ultimately, I chose to keep going. I'm glad I did! My first lucid dream occurred after ninety days of journaling and focusing, and they have steadily increased in frequency ever since.

If you answered this question A or B, you're already comfortable with programs that require a sustained effort over a long period of time before benefits become apparent. (Weight loss and exercise programs come to mind—but don't let a failed diet or two keep you from pursuing lucid dreams!) If you answered this question D or E, you may want to consider whether your interest in lucid dreaming is strong enough to sustain you through a program that may require sixty or ninety days to complete.

15. When you set long-term goals, how often do you achieve them?

Question 14 looks at how often you've been involved in long-term programs; Question 15 examines your success rate.

When you set out to lose fifteen pounds, were you successful? When you decided to go back to school to get that degree ... did you graduate? Last year, when you chose to start putting money away for that new car, did you make the sacrifices needed to make that down payment? When you bought into that financial self-help program that promised a "money makeover," did you reduce your debt over the course of the next year?

If you answered this question D or E, don't beat yourself up. Past successes boost your confidence and tenacity, making it easier to set and achieve new long-term goals. If you haven't had much success with long-term goals in the past, you can still experience success with this program, especially if you're willing to pursue your lucid dreaming goals with dedication and discipline.

16. How important is it for you to have a lucid dream?

This question essentially asks, "On a scale from one to five, with five being the most important, how important is it for you to have a lucid dream?"

Clearly, those who are more interested in pursuing lucid dreams are more likely to invest the time and energy required to generate them. At the same time, you very likely have a number of priorities—including, for example, paying bills and buying groceries—that probably outweigh lucid dreams in their relative importance to the quality of your life.

All of this to say: keep things in perspective. Several researchers have noted that people who strain to achieve lucid dreams have a much more difficult time generating them! Relax! Enjoy the journey! When it comes to lucidity, obsession is most likely a road to frustration.

On the other hand, if you answered E ("Not important at all"), you've either acquired a superhuman Zen-like detachment from your goals . . . or you're reading the wrong book!

17. How vivid do your non-lucid dreams tend to be?

When I interviewed other lucid dreamers, almost all of them told me their dreams had always tended to be extremely vivid and realistic. Most reported a tendency to dream in color. Many emphasized that their dreams incorporated a high degree of sensory texture, telling me in great detail about the atmospheric sounds, rough stones, chilly drafts, intense pleasure or pain, and hypnotic flavors they had experienced in their dreams.

My own dreams, too, have always been extremely vivid, incorporating a level of detail that astounds even me. A glance at my dream journal reveals a rich tapestry of realism: thriving cafes, shady forest trails teeming with wildlife, crowds peopled with individuals whose dress, speech, and mannerisms suggest they possess complex life histories.

In my experience, vivid dreamers have an easier time becoming lucid dreamers. And, of course, if your own dreams tend to be extremely vivid, you may have an easier time recognizing the dream cues (signs that help distinguish a dream from reality) that most lucid dreamers use as a tool for extending their consciousness into their dreams.

18. How frequently do you use visualizations— vivid, detailed imaginary pictures of something you desire—as a way of encouraging you to achieve your goals?

My own work with meditation has incorporated extensive use of visualization: picturing a future event as vividly and completely as possible. Later in this book, I discuss a variety of ways I've used visualizations (I call them "active daydreams") over the years. I'm convinced that this extension of my conscious mind into my imagination has made it easier for me to extend my conscious mind into the dreaming state.

Long before self-help gurus were charging $500 a pop to tell workshop participants to "picture their moment of success," magicians and metaphysicians were using visualization as a way of focusing both attention and intention. Seeing yourself succeeding can boost motivation and keep your efforts on track . . . and it can also introduce you to the thrill of manipulating a mental reality in ways that suit your personal tastes!

If you regularly visualize what you want as a way of encouraging success, or even if you spend a lot of time daydreaming, you're already skilled at producing and watching your own mental movies. If you answered this question D or E, you might try working with visualization as you pursue lucidity, as these skills clearly complement each other.

19. How frequently do impossible or unusual things (flight, sudden transformations, etc.) happen in your non-lucid dreams?

In dreams, we achieve the impossible on a regular basis. In one recent dream, frustrated by a long line at the cash register, I floated up to the ceiling like a helium balloon, drifted over the heads of distracted shoppers, and plopped myself at the head of the line. Just last week, a friend told me about a dream that featured a package that became, in rapid succession, a puppy, a baby, and a sack of freshly picked corn.

In our dreams both of us took our own impossible events—my impromptu flight and her package's remarkable transformations—in stride. You've very likely done the same thing in dreams of your own. In dreams, we frequently experience the impossible—and, strangely, even as we witness things that defy the laws of reality . . . we shrug them off as perfectly normal!

Each of these impossibilities represents an opportunity: a chance to realize, "Hey, this can't happen in the real world!" If your dreams are filled with things that can't happen or can't exist in the waking universe, you'll have more opportunities to realize you're dreaming and more opportunities to take control of your dreams.

20. How often has the appearance of an odd or "out of place" person, place, or thing alerted you to the fact that you were dreaming?

At first, Questions 19 and 20 look very similar . . . but in fact, Question 20 is probing for one very specific, very important event.

As I just mentioned, when dreaming, we frequently experience—and fail to be impressed by—impossible events. For reasons we don't yet clearly understand, dreamers readily accept bizarre events that, if they occurred in the waking world, would strike us as, at the very least, unsettling.

Many of the lucid dreamers I spoke with reported that, before having lucid dreams, they regularly

   a) witnessed impossible events,

   b) recognized these events as impossible, and

   c) realized they were dreaming.

Frequently, the shock of realization ("I'm dreaming!") woke them up. I've experienced this, too. In one dream, one of two friends at a café table suddenly vanished. It suddenly occurred to me that I was in a dream ... and that my vanishing friend must have disappeared because, having had the same insight, he had been thrown from the dream back into the real world. The moment this became clear— the same happened to me!

Recognizing the dream state is the first step toward achieving control of your dreams. If this happens to you frequently, you're well on your way to becoming a lucid dreamer.

Chapter 3 in a Nutshell

Lucid dreaming is a skill; with dedication and discipline, almost anyone can have a lucid dream. The Lucid Dreaming Profile explores your sleeping habits, the quality of your sleep, the nature of your dreams, and your current level of control over dreams and dream recall. While it's not a scientific tool, the LDP can help you estimate the amount of time and effort you may have to invest in order to achieve lucid dreams of your own. It may also help you identify changes you can make in your sleeping habits or nightly routines that will encourage lucid dreaming.

What's Next?

Your LDP score gives you some idea of just how easily you may engineer lucid dreams of your own. Completing the profile may also help you identify small changes in your lifestyle or routine that can greatly increase your chances of achieving lucidity.

With the profile completed, you have several options:

- Chapter 4 provides an overview of the ongoing research into lucid dreams. If you're curious about the growing body of scientific evidence supporting the reality of lucid dreaming (or if you're dealing with skeptics who are dismissive of the idea), this chapter is a great place to begin.

- If you're ready to start your own lucid dreaming regimen, you may wish to skip to chapter 5, "Mr. Sandman, Bring Me a (Lucid) Dream." In that chapter, you'll gain hands-on experience with the tools and techniques that will put you on the fast track to lucidity.

four

Lucid Dreaming
in the Lab

In this chapter, you'll discover:

- The arguments skeptics use to dismiss lucid dreaming as pure fantasy
- The vast amount of literature testifying to the reality of lucid dreaming
- The research of Stephen LaBerge, the premier lucid dreaming researcher
- The objective evidence supporting the existence of lucid dreaming as a real and measurable state of altered consciousness

Does Lucid Dreaming Exist?

Is there really even such a thing as a lucid dream?

For those of us who regularly experience lucidity, this question sounds positively silly. Of course there are lucid dreams! "Just last night," you say, "as I was dreaming of talking to my friend Dennis, I suddenly realized Dennis was still the same age he was the last time I saw him, thirty years ago. Right away, I knew I was dreaming, so I changed Dennis into that plumber from *Desperate Housewives* and took my own little trip down Wisteria Lane!"

And maybe you did. But how can you *prove* you brought your *Desperate Housewives* fantasy to life? There's no video. We don't yet have technology capable of capturing images from the dreaming brain. Isn't it possible that, instead of being in control of your dream, you simply *dreamed* that you were in control of your dream? Or that you were confused? Or deluded? Or that you're lying?

In other words: if you had to prove that lucid dreaming exists, what objective evidence could you cite to support your claim to lucidity?

Acerbic Assertions vs. Transcendent Truths

As noted in chapter 1, skeptics such as Robert Todd Carroll, who continue to assert that the lucid state is a figment of the dreamer's imagination, often employ ridicule and contempt when attacking the idea of lucidity.[1] Perhaps an aversion to

---

1 Robert Todd Carroll, *The Skeptic's Dictionary*, s.v. "lucid dreaming," http://skepdic.com/lucdream.html (accessed February 2, 2006).

this kind of treatment has led some lucid dreaming authors and experts to distance themselves entirely from objective research. Rather than defend their beliefs or seek evidence to support the existence of the lucid state, these lucid dreamers warn readers away from those who would take a scientific approach. Robert Moss, in *Conscious Dreaming: A Spiritual Path for Everyday Life* (1996), writes, "There are no 'experts' on dreams. ... If you need guidance, seek it from frequent fliers, not academics who put plate glass between their experiments and their experience."

On the one hand, we have a skeptic claiming lucid dreams are little more than New Age hooey. On the other, we have a true believer asserting that we have little or nothing to gain from scientific inquiry into lucid dreaming phenomena. As we will see, a growing body of evidence—much of it based on laboratory studies of lucid dreamers in action—challenges both of these conclusions.

Expert Testimony vs. Evidence

Believers in astral projection, out-of-body experiences, and remote viewing must currently take a great deal on faith. The evidence supporting these phenomena remains deeply personal and almost entirely anecdotal. Laboratory evidence on these subjects is scant or nonexistent; almost all the information we have comes from the testimony of those who claim to achieve the state.

For many years, this was also the case with lucid dreaming. The Marquis d'Hervey de Saint-Denys' book *Dreams and How to Guide Them* (1867) was an extensive chronicle spanning twenty years of the author's adventures with lucid dreaming. Skeptics would be quick (and correct) to point out that such a book, as one man's personal testimony, would not carry the weight of scientific evidence.

While Sigmund Freud neglected to mention lucid dreaming in his masterwork *The Interpretation of Dreams*, he did add, in a second edition published in 1909, a note that seems to refer to lucid dreams:

> [T]here are some people who are quite clearly aware during the night that they are asleep and dreaming and who thus seem to possess the faculty of consciously directing their dreams. If, for instance, a dreamer of this kind is dissatisfied with the turn taken by a dream, he can break it off without waking up and start it again in another direction—just as a popular dramatist may under pressure give his play a happier ending.

Here, Freud seems to acknowledge that certain people can and do achieve consciousness and control while dreaming . . . but such an acknowledgment, even on the part of a highly respected authority, cannot be considered as objective evidence that lucid dreams exist.

In *Lucid Dreaming* (1985), Stephen LaBerge lists a number of authors, doctors, researchers, and occultists who have recorded and published their personal experiences with lucid dreams: Ernst Mach, Frederik van Eeden, Yves Delage, Mary Arnold-Forster, Hugh Calloway, Piotr D. Ouspensky, Aiwani Embury Brown, Harold von Moers-Messmer, and Nathan Rapport among them. At best, though, the books and articles produced by these dreamers are only descriptions of the lucid state. As such, these testimonies remain vulnerable to the skeptical claim that lucid dreams are little more than "dreams in which the dreamer dreams he knows he is dreaming."

The First Objective Evidence of Lucidity

It's relatively easy to verify whether or not an experimental subject is asleep. Activity in the sleeping brain differs dramatically from activity in the waking brain. Sensitive instruments—EEG monitors, in particular—can record and verify these differences.

It's also relatively easy to determine whether or not a sleeping subject is dreaming. Almost all of us have seen partners, children, or pets in the throes of a nocturnal adventure. We've seen the twitching limbs and rolling eyes—both of which indicate a dream is in progress. Visual observation, paired with recordings of brain activity, can provide irrefutable proof that the laboratory subject is both asleep and dreaming.

The challenge facing lucid dream researchers, however, was not to prove that the dream state existed, but that a *conscious* dream state existed. Of course, laboratory subjects could attest to their success in assuming control of their dreams, but only anecdotally and only after the fact. During REM sleep, when lucid dreams take place, the human body is paralyzed. So how could a dreamer, while still in a dream, communicate his lucid state to the outside world?

The Eyes Have It

Though he has oddly chosen to draw very little attention to his work, Keith Hearne, a British parapsychologist at Liverpool University, was very likely the first researcher to solve this problem. As early as 1978, Hearne hit upon the idea of training dreamers to use eye movements to signal their achievement of consciousness.[2]

Along with the respiratory system, the eyes do not seem to be subject to the creeping paralysis that prevents us from acting out our dreams. At least one earlier study had established that the movements of a dreamer's physical eyes corresponded to some degree to eye movements reported in a dream. (The eyes of the subject in question had been moving regularly from left to right while dreaming in a laboratory setting. When awakened, he told researchers he had been dreaming of a ping-pong match.) It seemed possible, then, that a dreamer might learn a set of specific eye movements in the waking world . . . and then, after achieving consciousness in the dreamworld, use those eye movements to signal his success.

Hearne's efforts, particularly with a subject named Alan Worsley, met with great success. Over the course of a year, Worsley spent forty-five nights in Hearne's sleep lab. While sleeping there, Worsley achieved eight lucid dreams. During each of them, even as instruments verified the fact he was asleep and dreaming, Worsley was able to signal his achieve-

---

2 K.M.T. Hearne, "Lucid Dreams: An Electrophysiological and Psychological Study" (PhD diss., University of Liverpool, 1978).

ment of lucidity using the eye movement "Morse Code" he had established with Hearne.

Further, when assigned simple "dream tasks" prior to falling asleep, Worsley could recall and perform those tasks in his lucid dreams. Once, Hearne asked Worsley to try drawing triangles on the walls of a dream room; when Worsley did so, his physical eyes followed the motion of his dream hand, executing a series of distinctive triangular movements. On another occasion, Worsley was asked to take a specific number of dream steps. While sleep paralysis prevented his physical legs from moving, Hearne recorded corresponding electrical impulses in Worsley's brain and legs.

Curiously, while Hearne chronicled these developments in his unpublished doctoral dissertation, he never took steps to draw the scientific community's attention to his groundbreaking work. Apart from an article he published in a minor British nursing magazine, Hearne seemed content to allow his work to remain relatively unknown.

Parallels Across the Pond

In the late 1970s, Stephen LaBerge, an American researcher, began his own quest to document the reality of the lucid dream state. Though completely unaware of Hearne's work, LaBerge hit on the very same idea: using eye movements as signals of consciousness. Unlike Hearne, LaBerge—a lifelong lucid dreamer—elected to use himself as a subject.

On Friday the 13th, 1978, LaBerge achieved his first lucid dream in a laboratory setting:

The image of what seemed to be the instruction booklet for a vacuum cleaner or some such appliance floated by. It struck me as mere flotsam on the stream of consciousness, but as I focused on it and tried to read the writing, the image gradually stabilized and I had the sensation of opening my (dream) eyes. ... I decided to do the eye movements that we had agreed upon as a signal. I moved my finger in a vertical line in front of me, following it with my eyes. (*Lucid Dreaming*, 1980)

When LaBerge awoke, he discovered "two large eye movements on the polygraph record"—proof positive that, while experiencing REM sleep, he had been able to send a deliberate signal back to the waking world.

Those two spikes on the polygraph were just the beginning. In LaBerge's laboratory, he and other lucid dreamers—dubbed *oneironauts*, or dream sailors—would conduct the experiments that, slowly but surely, would define the rules that govern lucidity.

More Insights from the Lab

Over time, LaBerge, his students, and other researchers would document aspects of the lucid dreaming experience that remain remarkably consistent from dreamer to dreamer.

The Physiology of Lucidity

Essentially, a dreamer has two bodies—a physical body, which is paralyzed while sleeping, and a dream body, through which dream experiences are sensed and dream actions are carried out. Very early in their research, LaBerge and his students discovered that these two bodies appear to be intimately linked. In other words, what we experience in our dream bodies has a very real—and measurable—impact on our apparently passive physical bodies.

Movement. Our physical eyes mirror the movements of their dream counterparts. Moving dream arms and legs will send impulses to our physical arms and legs, but most of these are dampened or repressed by sleep paralysis.

Brain activity. When lucid dreamers sing songs or count aloud in their dreams, this activity accesses the portions of the brain that govern musical and mathematical capability in the real world.

Respiration. In one experiment, lucid dreamers were asked to send two signals: one when they achieved lucidity, and another when they began, in the dream, to hold their breath. Outside observers reviewing a printout of the dreamer's physiological states were able to pinpoint the occurrence of the agreed-upon eye signals and the point at which the dreamers' efforts to hold their breath prompted their physical bodies to suspend normal breathing.

Sex. One of the first indulgences of many lucid dreamers is dream sex. And why not? In a lucid dream, a dreamer can have any kind of sex with anyone, anytime, anywhere, without any concern for pregnancy or sexually transmitted disease.

Lab volunteers, instructed to send signals marking the beginning of lucidity, the assumption of dream sex, and the achievement of dream orgasm helped researchers verify that the sleeping physical body responds to dream sex exactly as it would to sex in the real world (with the odd exception of heart rate, which appears unaffected). During dream sex, a lucid dreamer's breath rate increases. Males experience erections; females experience increased vaginal blood flow and contractions.

While dream orgasms do not always result in ejaculation, both male and female lucid dreamers report that sexual activity in lucid dreams often leads to overwhelmingly powerful orgasms. (Yet another reason to try lucid dreaming!)

Lucidity and Consciousness
MEMORY

Once lucid dreamers become aware they are dreaming, they can, with practice, easily recall instructions memorized in the waking world. Their success in doing so indicates that our consciousness in the dreamworld has intimate ties with our waking consciousness.

That said, the dream state does appear to impair or distort certain aspects of memory:

- In experiments conducted by B. G. Marcot and described by Celia Green, volunteers who have memorized long strings of numbers—including the value of pi to several digits—report that, during lucid dreams, they are unable to recall more than the first six or seven numbers in the sequence.[3]

---

3 Ceila Green, *Lucid Dreaming: The Paradox of Consciousness during Sleep* (New York: Routledge, 1994), 44.

- Even in lucid dreams, dreamers frequently fail to notice anything unusual about the appearance of dead relatives or long lost friends. As one dreamer noted to me in an email, "After I woke up, of course, I realized I was talking to my sister, who had been dead for seven years. In the dream, though—even though I was in control of other aspects—it never occurred to me that she was dead. I had forgotten that completely."

- Though lucid dreams are unusually intense and vivid, they, too, can be difficult to move from short-term to long-term memory. Unless dreamers are careful to record details of their dreams, their experiences will become more difficult to recall with time in ways that events in the waking world do not.

THE SENSE OF TIME

In LaBerge's lab, lucid dreamers have successfully slipped into the dream state, achieved consciousness, and then performed various counting tasks. By moving their eyes in time with their count, dreamers are able to signal their perception of the passage of time within the dream universe.

Many people, in an effort to explain why dreams fade so quickly or how they can seem to last so long, have suggested that dreams take place at high speeds. LaBerge's timing experiments, though, suggest that dreamtime passes at roughly the same rate as waking time—at least when dreamers are lucid.

A Sense of the Waking World

A dreamer is not completely cut off from physical reality. Almost all of us have experienced, at some point or another, the integration of waking-world events into the dreamscape:

- A song playing on the alarm clock becomes a song played by a performer in our dream.

- In our dream, a ringing telephone in the waking world can be heard, muffled and distant, as though coming from an adjacent room.

- If a spouse, partner, or roommate calls your name, you may hear that voice in the dream (and may, in a variety of ways, work that person or message into the dreamscape).

Lucid dreamers, too, freely incorporate stimuli from the real world into their dreams—a fact that has both aided and complicated lucid dreaming research.

One of the primary hurdles to lucid dreaming is the dreamer's tendency to deny the dream state—to accept the events of a dream, no matter how unlikely or bizarre they are, as events in the waking world. But what if sleepers, monitored by computers in the waking world, could be given a subtle signal when REM sleep begins? If so, could receiving such a signal help dreamers achieve lucidity more quickly and easily?

LaBerge and his team eventually developed a series of specialized sleep masks—now discontinued—sold variously as the Dreamlight, Dreamlink, and NovaDreamer. When sensors in these masks detected the onset of rapid eye movements, lights positioned over the dreamer's eyes flickered on and off. Researchers reasoned that dreamers would sense the flickering light, remember they were asleep, and achieve consciousness within the dream state.

In many cases, the illuminated masks worked well. But subjects also reported a special challenge associated with their use: all too often, the signal would be incorporated into the events of the dream—as fireworks, for example, or as a brilliant sunset. As a result, dreamers would fail to recognize the cue . . . and fail to achieve lucidity, as well.

The Persistence of Personal Morality

LaBerge's volunteers reported that, despite efforts to do so in the interests of science, they had difficulty visualizing or carrying out morally repugnant tasks in their lucid dreams.

I experienced this in my own pursuit of lucid dreams. In the waking world, fidelity to my life partner is very important to me; in fact, I go out of my way to avoid any action that could be interpreted as disrespectful of our relationship.

As I began to achieve lucidity, I was naturally curious about the possibility of bringing certain fantasies to life. Again and again, though, even when opportunities would present themselves, I would decline, explaining to dream paramours that I was happily taken and, therefore, unavailable.

LaBerge's work—and my own experience—suggests that deep-seated aspects of our personal morality tend to be carried over into our dreams.

Connections with Spirituality

Throughout lucid dream literature—whether published by LaBerge or others—you will find references to lucid dreams as deeply spiritual events.

This connection with a profound sense of the spiritual may not be expressed in purely mystical terms, but its influence is undeniable. Dreamers repeatedly describe the lucid state as joyful, transcendent, or transformational. Some report feeling a greater sense of connection and unity with both the dreamscape and, after awakening, reality. The "high" experienced during a lucid dream frequently carries over into the waking world, leaving the lucid dreamer feeling happier, more fulfilled, and more centered throughout the day.

This effect has led a number of advocates and authors to associate lucid dreaming with everything from out-of-body experiences to shamanism. While you may or may not be interested in using lucid dreaming as a connection to the spiritual realm, knowing that others frequently make such connections can prepare you for the profound emotional and psychological impact of the lucid experience.

The Laws of Lucidity

While the dreamscape defies the rules and regulations of reality, LaBerge and his team have documented that the universe in which lucid dreams occur does operate according to its own, internally consistent set of rules.

Unstable text, odd clocks, and broken light switches. For reasons as yet undetermined, text (signs, menus, newspaper headlines, posters, and so forth) and timepieces (clocks and watches) are rarely consistent or reliable during lucid dreams. This effect is so widespread, lucid dreamers have adopted it as a fairly certain means of reality testing. Try it now: look at a clock (or even the text of this book), glance away, and look back. Does the clock report the same time? Is the text on this page consistent? If so, you're very likely awake.

Light switches, too, can be used for reality testing. While they work reliably in the real world, within the dreamscape they often fail to work—or work in strange or unexpected ways (by producing water, for example, or by breaking off in the dreamer's hands).

Magical imagination. In the real world, the things we imagine don't often appear, solid and fully realized, before our eyes. In the lucid dreamscape, however, it can be very difficult to imagine something without causing it to happen. Generally, when lucid dreamers picture something in their minds, the dreamscape shifts to incorporate their mental image.

"Changing channels" by covering "dream eyes." A number of lucid dreamers have reported an ability to "change channels"—significantly alter a dream or switch from one dream to another—by placing their dream hands over their dream eyes.

Before reading about this technique, I had discovered it myself. Especially when just learning to lucid dream, my lucid state would slowly "slip away," and, instead of controlling the events of my dream, I would be caught up in them. Eventually, I learned that I could avoid a loss of lucidity by shielding my dream eyes from distracting or unexpected events. If something or someone unwelcome appeared, the act of covering my dream eyes for a moment would delete the intrusive material and remind me that I was in control.

Adaptation to dream cues. Lucid dreamers often select dream cues—events that, because they happen often in dreams, can be taken as a sign that a dream is in progress. My own dream cues include rides in elevators (which are usually oversized or which malfunction in some way), skyscrapers and towers, and, for reasons I cannot fathom, celebrity cameos. When confronted by these things, whether in dreams or in the waking world, I always pause and ask, "Am I dreaming?"

Some volunteers, however, report that, with time, they adapt to dream cues. Sometimes, dreamers will, for reasons unknown, stop recognizing well-established dream cues; other times, the cues simply stop appearing in dreams.[4]

This eventual "desensitization" to dream cues is yet another reason to keep a dream journal. Reviewing a record of your dreams over time will help you detect recurring themes and repeating events—good candidates for dream cues. As you become desensitized to certain cues, your dream journal will provide you with the information you need to identify new ones.

---

4 Ibid., 20.

Lucidity as a Skill

Perhaps the most useful insight gleaned from LaBerge's work is the verification of the concept that lucid dreaming is a skill that almost anyone can learn.

MOTIVATION AS A FACTOR

How badly do you want to have lucid dreams? Your answer to that question may, in the end, be the very best predictor of how likely you are to have one.

LaBerge noticed early on that degree of motivation has a direct correlation with lucid dreaming success. In my own work, and in correspondence with a number of other lucid dreamers, I have also found this to be the case. When I half-heartedly pursued lucid dreams in my college days, I achieved very little. Years later, when I made a long-term commitment to the process, I experienced quick success.

INDUCTION TECHNIQUES

In addition to noting the impact of motivation, LaBerge documented a number of highly effective techniques for inducing lucid dreams:

- *Reality Testing.* Covered in detail in other parts of this book, reality checks—simple tests designed to determine whether you're in the waking world or the dream state—proved to be a powerful tool for inducing lucidity.

- *Early Waking.* For reasons not clearly understood, the last ninety minutes of sleep are prime time for lucid dreaming. LaBerge and others, in an effort to take advantage of this, developed a practice of waking up early, spending thirty to forty-five minutes awake, and returning to bed. This simple practice—if you can tolerate it—appears very likely to produce lucid dreams.

- *Mnemonics.* MILD—the Mnemonic Induction of Lucid Dreams—is a strategy LaBerge developed early in his research and used with great personal success. Adherents, whenever they awaken from a dream, pause to recall the events of the dream in as much detail as possible. As they fall asleep again, they mentally repeat a dream affirmation, such as "Next time I'm dreaming, I'll know I'm dreaming." Finally, as they slip into sleep, they deliberately imagine themselves seeing a dream cue and recognizing a lucid dream.

The Lucidity Institute

LaBerge's work continues today through The Lucidity Institute (TLI). Founded by LaBerge, TLI promotes lucid dreaming, teaches a number of lucid dreaming techniques, and positions lucid dreaming as a practice with the potential to enhance emotional health and personal well-being.

In its early years, the efforts of TLI included great emphasis on dedicated software and hardware—expensive products designed to make lucid dreams easier to achieve. The aforementioned Dreamlight, Dreamlink, and NovaDreamer masks, along with a number of other devices designed to alert sleepers to the onset of REM sleep, were offered as high-tech solutions for those who hoped to have lucid dreams of their own.

Today, however, these products appear to have fallen out of fashion. While these and similar devices are still offered (new or used) by third-party vendors, TLI has distanced itself from technology as a learning strategy. LaBerge's latest book assures readers that, while these devices are useful, they are by no means necessary. Today, TLI emphasizes retreats and workshops (such as "Dreaming and Awakening: A 10-Day Residential Training Program in Lucid Dreaming and Dream Yoga") as a means of personal transformation; the organization's web site (www.lucidity.com) serves as a community hub where lucid dreamers participate in forums and submit dream records for use in various Institute-sponsored experiments.

Pursuing the Evidence: Why Bother?

Generally speaking, having a lucid dream of your very own is probably the best way to prove to yourself that lucid dreams exist.

That being the case, many people might feel justified in completely dismissing the need for a formal, scientific inquiry. "I've had a lucid dream," we might well say. "Why do I need science to prove what I already know is true?"

A growing body of evidence suggests that the lucid state is an objective reality. The real benefit of objective study, though, may have less to do with *proving* lucidity . . . and more to do with *applying* it. Laboratory efforts to study lucid dreaming may well provide the insights we need to

- make the skill of lucid dreaming easier to learn,
- learn more about the nature of consciousness,
- understand better how our consciousness impacts our experience of reality, and
- employ lucid dreams as a means of enhancing physical and emotional health in the waking world.

Chapter 4 in a Nutshell

For some people, no amount of evidence will ever prove the existence of lucid dreams. For others, evidence is irrelevant; their goal is the experience of lucidity, not the proof of it.

Increasingly, though, the existence of a "lucid state" is fast becoming more a matter of fact than faith. Even as instruments verify that the subjects are asleep and dreaming, lucid dreamers in the lab are consistently able to recall instructions, carry out tasks, and send feedback to the waking world. Further, thanks to the efforts of researchers such as Stephen LaBerge, the peculiar physiological and psychological laws governing the lucid state are being tested, mapped, and verified.

In the end, the biggest benefit gained from a scientific inquiry into lucid dreaming may not be "proof" of lucidity. Instead, through organizations like The Lucidity Institute, we may learn how everyday people can tap into the enormous potential of lucid dreams to enhance physical and emotional well-being.

What's Next?

If you're the type of reader who needed an overview of the evidence before launching your own investigation into lucid dreaming, now may be the perfect time to double back to read earlier chapters, taking the Guided Tour of Sleep in chapter 2 ("To Sleep, Perchance to Dream") or completing the Lucid Dreaming Profile (chapter 3).

If you're ready to pursue lucid dreams of your own, you should continue to chapter 5, "Mr. Sandman, Bring Me a (Lucid) Dream."

five

Mr. Sandman, Bring Me a (Lucid) Dream

In this chapter, you'll discover:

- How finding a "dream buddy" in the waking world can enhance your quest for lucidity
- How meditation, affirmation, and visualization can be used as effective lucid dreaming tools
- Why small changes in your sleep patterns make lucid dreams more likely to occur
- What kinds of objects make effective "dream tokens"—and why

Encouraging Lucid Dreams

Once you decide you'd like to experience lucid dreaming for yourself, you have two options:

- Wait around for a random lucid dream to occur.
- Start practicing some techniques designed to boost your chances of having a lucid dream.

If you're reading this book, you're probably not the sort of person who prefers to sit around and wait for luck to bring a lucid dream her way ... so this chapter provides straightforward techniques for encouraging lucid dreams. In it, I cover a number of techniques that have worked for me and for many other lucid dreamers. You don't have to adopt them all (I didn't), but each one you *do* adopt will greatly enhance your chances of experiencing lucidity.

Dream Buddies

At first, you might think a dream buddy is a friend who appears exclusively in your dreams. In fact, dream buddies are friends in the *waking* world—friends who share your interest in lucid dreams and who are going through this program at the same time as you. You'll have a lot more fun learning to achieve lucidity when you share your goals, your efforts, and your victories with like-minded folks.

As you may already know from dieting or exercising, the more enjoyable a program is, the more likely you are to stick with it. Maintaining a lucid dreaming regimen for sixty to ninety days is a challenge for anyone. If your enthusiasm or dedication begins to droop, a dream buddy can encourage you to stick with the program.

Partners, spouses, husbands, wives, and roommates make great dream buddies. First, they're accessible: you're very likely to see these people on a regular basis. Breakfast time is a great time to share dreams and discuss results. Best of all, pursuing lucid dreams with someone you care about can make the entire experience more meaningful.

No partner? No problem. A close friend—preferably, someone who doesn't mind getting an excited "I just had a lucid dream!" update in the middle of the night—will work just as well.

Affirmations

Self-help programs of all kinds use affirmations—strong, positive statements of intention—as a way of reprogramming the mind. Just before each meal, a dieter might tell himself, "I enjoy making healthier choices." A high-powered sales executive might post a strip of paper on her bathroom mirror that says, "I earn $120,000 in commissions each year." A person seeking better control of his temper might intone, "I slow down and breathe before taking action" as part of his morning routine.

Affirmations take advantage of the fact that our thoughts have tremendous potential to shape our actions ... and our lives. They're a powerful tool for shifting attention and changing behavior. As you pursue lucid dreams, there are three kinds of affirmations you may find useful.

Positive Affirmations

Positive affirmations are bold statements designed to re-inforce your intention to have a lucid dream. When using positive affirmations, you should always

- speak slowly and clearly;
- speak your affirmation aloud;
- phrase your affirmation in a positive way, as though your desire is already a reality;
- exude confidence;
- use brief, simple statements of your intention;
- use the same affirmation again and again;
- face yourself in the mirror, if possible, when making your affirmation.

Some great affirmations for lucid dreamers include:

- I look forward to being a lucid dreamer.
- I recognize when I am dreaming.
- I take control of my dreams.
- I remember my dreams.
- I look forward to my next lucid dream.

If you print these affirmations out, you can stick them on bathroom mirrors, rearview mirrors (without obstructing your vision, of course), makeup mirrors, notebook covers, key ring fobs, or the back of your iPod—anywhere you'll see them several times throughout the day. If you use a computer, you can use an affirmation as your screensaver or wallpaper. If your cell phone allows custom wallpaper, you can place your affirmation there, too. If you're alone when you see the affirmation, say it out loud.

When you first begin using affirmations, you may feel a little strange announcing your intentions to the universe. There are good reasons, though, for saying affirmations aloud—and all of them have to do with a remarkable ability possessed by every human being: the power of association.

First, by assuming a confident posture and tone when making your lucid dreaming affirmation, your body learns to associate the idea of lucid dreaming with the feeling of confidence. The more often you reinforce this confidence/lucid dreaming connection, the stronger it becomes. The result? Your confidence with regard to lucid dreaming grows . . . and, when you have a lucid dream, that feeling of confidence returns.

In addition, saying your affirmation aloud dispels both fear and doubt. The whole purpose of an affirmation is to send a clear message to your subconscious mind: *I am a lucid dreamer*. What message are you sending your subconscious if you murmur, whisper, or mutter your affirmation? What associations will you make if you allow yourself to feel embarrassed or self-conscious about speaking your affirmations aloud?

Meditative Affirmations

Especially when used in conjunction with positive affirmations, meditative affirmations can be an extremely powerful tool in your lucid dreaming arsenal. Because they are repeated when your mind is relaxed and open, meditative affirmations easily cross the barrier between your conscious and unconscious minds.

You can easily adapt positive affirmations for use as meditative affirmations. Here's a simple, step-by-step method for using them to boost your lucid dreaming potential:

- Schedule ten to fifteen minutes a day to dedicate to your meditation practice. If possible, schedule your meditation session at the same time every day. Normally, in order to keep from dropping off to sleep while meditating, you would avoid scheduling your meditation first thing in the morning or right before bed. For our purposes, especially if meditation relaxes you or makes you feel sleepy, meditating just before going to bed is fine.

- Choose a comfortable, secluded place for your meditation. If sitting on the floor hurts your back, sit with your back against the foot of your bed (or sit in a comfortable chair). If you live with others who might unintentionally distract you, alert them to your routine and ask for calls and other interruptions to be held until your meditation is done. (You might also find a signal—a tassel to hang on a doorknob, for example—that will warn others that your meditation is in progress.) If you can't find a quiet space, try masking out distracting noises with a fan, a tabletop fountain, or headphones.

- Begin your meditation by slowing down. For the first several minutes, simply close your eyes and monitor (but do not try to regulate) your breathing. When your breath and pulse begin to slow, you may want to use any of several meditative techniques to deepen your relaxation. You might, for example, imagine inhaling a white light until your body glows with energy. Alternatively, you might picture a gentle, white glow descending from the crown of your head, down the length of your body, to the soles of your feet. As the light progresses, allow the muscles it touches to relax and go limp.

- When you are completely relaxed, call one of your lucid dreaming affirmations to mind. While your mind is still and receptive, see the affirmation projected on the inside of your eyelids. Some people very gently "think it aloud" at this point; others prefer to see it without mentally voicing it.

- Emphasize the affirmation in time with your breathing. Think or see the first half as you inhale, and then think or see the second half as you exhale.

- Conclude your meditation. Let your affirmation go. With a clear mind, open yourself to whatever happens. Resolve to be excited about and at peace with it. After following your breathing for a few minutes, slowly open your eyes and return to wakefulness.

As you work with positive and meditative affirmations, remember that the process should be a positive and gentle one. Remember the old Seinfeld episode in which people who wanted a serene state of mind stormed around screaming, "Serenity Now!"? Beating yourself up with affirmations (or using demanding affirmations, such as "I *will* have a lucid dream!" or "I *must* become a lucid dreamer!") will only hinder your progress.

Prayer

Prayer may already be a part of your daily routine (some, in fact, view prayer as a highly stylized form of affirmation). If you do pray, especially if you make a habit of bringing your hopes and aspirations into your prayers, you should consider praying about lucid dreaming.

Requests made through prayer work best when they are kept very simple. While addressing your prayers to the Higher Power appropriate to your spiritual traditions, mention your desire to begin having lucid dreams. As with affirmations, you should avoid demands. Instead, a simple "I'm excited about lucid dreaming, and I trust you to help me achieve my goal" will do.

Especially if you pray just before going to sleep, you may find praying about lucid dreaming is a relaxing, powerful way to increase the likelihood of having a lucid dream. When your first lucid dream occurs, be sure to offer a prayer of thanks and celebration!

Be Consistent!

While I do hear from people who have, after just one day of affirmation, achieved their first lucid dream, such immediate results are rare. It can be very difficult for success-oriented people to realize that communicating with the subconscious mind takes a great deal of time and discipline. You may affirm your intention for thirty, sixty, or even ninety days without results.

The key, of course, is consistency. You're not in a race; there are no prizes or merit awards for "having a first lucid dream after only four days of trying." That said, if you establish your affirmation routine and stick with it, you dramatically increase the odds of having a lucid dream.

Visualizations

Visualizations are essentially daydreams on steroids: vivid mental movies that depict the achievement of a goal. Athletic coaches regularly use visualization as a coaching tool. It's not unusual for a softball coach to tell a struggling player to "see the bat make contact with the ball" in her mind. Dancers speak of mental rehearsals: seeing a perfected performance in their mind's eye. Sales reps often picture a successful sales call in meticulous detail before ever knocking on a single door.

Throughout my career as a trainer, public speaker, and writer, I've made extensive use of the power of visualization. Before teaching a class, I teach it at least twice—from start to finish—in my mind. I can't tell you how often this process has allowed me to identify problematic material, refine activities, and improve examples. My virtual students frequently surprise me with questions and responses that preview those my real students ask later on. Teaching a course or rehearsing a speech in my head helps me feel more comfortable with the material and more confident when delivering it.

You can call on the power of visualization anytime, anywhere: on airline flights, in waiting rooms, on long drives . . . anytime you have an opportunity to turn your focus inward. With a little time, imagination, and practice, you can produce vivid mental movies—complete with a stirring musical sound track and expensive special effects—that allow you to foresee your own success.

When you integrate visualizations into your pursuit of lucid dreams, you can make dramatic strides forward with very small investments of time and effort. Some tips:

- Visualize yourself preparing for bed. Go through your routine in detail: showering, brushing teeth, brushing your hair—whatever you do. Slip between the sheets. See yourself closing your eyes and drifting off to sleep. See a smile form on your face as you begin your lucid dream.

- Visualize yourself having a lucid dream. See yourself in a dream situation: on a beach, in a classroom, at your office—anywhere. Imagine that you notice one small detail that's wrong—a dream cue that gives away the fact that the world around you is not a part of normal reality. (Perhaps a seashell rings like a cell phone, or a poster on the wall says different things every time you read it.) Allow yourself to experience the excited rush of recognition. Then, pick an activity you hope to experience in lucid dreams: flying, perhaps, or visiting with a friend or family member who has passed away. See yourself summoning the experience, see it take place, and relish your sense of satisfaction at having achieved your goal.

- Visualize yourself excitedly telling a friend about your lucid dreaming experience. Relate your lucid dream in detail. Share your excitement and satisfaction, and allow your friend to express interest . . . or even envy! As a bonus, pretend that, as you speak to your friend, he or she suddenly changes into someone else—a sure sign that you are dreaming. Take advantage of the moment and call up one of your favorite lucid dream scenarios and live it to the fullest.

Some people prefer guided visualizations: picturing in detail what someone else reads or describes aloud. If you like the idea of a guided visualization, you can always write down what you want to visualize, record it, and play it back on your computer, a CD player, or your iPod.

I used visualizations extensively while pursuing my first lucid dream. If you have difficulty coming up with your own visualization scenarios, you can always adapt mine. You might also consider reading the following passage aloud and using it as a guided visualization:

It's late, and after a long, productive day, I'm getting ready for bed. I look forward to being in bed. I enjoy the feeling of cool, soft sheets. I look forward to sleep.

The room is quiet. The lights are low. I'm already drowsy. I climb into bed, taking just seconds to settle into my favorite position. I feel completely safe, completely relaxed. My mind is calm and clear. Almost before I know it, my eyes close and my breathing slows. Seconds later, I drift off to sleep.

My sleep is deep and restful. Slowly, slowly, I rise from deep sleep, drifting upward, like a bubble in water. I feel myself edging over into REM sleep. As a dream begins, I see my eyelids shift back and forth, back and forth. In my mind's eye, I can see a peaceful garden, soaked in sunlight. The cool breeze is perfumed with the crisp scent of evergreen trees. I hear birds overhead and a fountain in the distance. Paths go off in all directions.

A butterfly lights gently on my hand. As I watch, the patterns on its wings shift, changing from red and yellow diamonds to blue and orange stars. Immediately, I realize I've never seen a butterfly like this one, and I suspect I'm in a dream.

The butterfly lifts away, gliding into the sky. Confident that I'm dreaming, I raise my face to the sky and try to follow it. Slowly, my feet lift off the ground. I open my eyes. I'm rising into the air, like a helium balloon. I discover with great joy that I can steer myself in any direction just by thinking about where I want to go. I know, now, that I'm in a dream and that I'm in absolute control of this incredible world.

Tonight, I decide I want to visit my childhood home. Even as I recall the details—the neighborhood, the street, the doorway, my bedroom—they fade into existence around me. I drift down to the floor and stand in the middle of my room. I spend several happy minutes exploring the room and rediscovering old memories.

When I'm ready to go, I release the room, and it turns into mist. I rise through the mist, incredibly happy that I've been able to have a lucid dream. I wake up in my own bed, completely rested and refreshed. When I get up, my feeling of accomplishment and confidence stays with me throughout the day.

Like affirmations, visualizations send powerful messages to your subconscious mind, clarifying your desires and spelling out your goals. As a potential lucid dreamer, you have another great reason for using visualizations: they give you extensive practice creating and assuming control of mental imagery! As you become more and more comfortable with the idea of authoring and directing your visualizations, you are building an association between the presence of vivid internal images and a persistent state of conscious control.

Downtime

Downtime is exactly what the name implies: a deliberate appointment with nothing at all. The goal of downtime is to allow your mind and body to shed the concerns of the day. Low lights and meditative music should be turned on. Televisions, cell phones, messaging devices, and computers should be turned off. Franklin Planners, DayTimers, and other reminders of the rat race should be put away.

Using this time for meditation—unless meditation energizes you—is a great idea. But don't get me wrong: your downtime doesn't have to be spent sitting idly in a chair. You can read a comforting book (thrillers are out, but Scripture, motivational reading, or pleasure reading is welcome). You can listen to a CD or MP3 of calming music. You can scrapbook, or put together that photo album you've always talked about, or browse travel magazines. You can soak yourself in a hot tub. You can relish a light snack.

Once you incorporate downtime into your life, you'll fight to keep it there—the impact is that dramatic. In addition to sleeping more soundly and dreaming more vividly, you'll enjoy keeping an eye out for "downtime indulgences": an aromatherapy candle to enjoy, a Liquid Mind CD, a tin of exquisite bath salts. A half-hour of downtime will make a huge difference in the quality of your sleep and dreams; a full hour is a decadent luxury.

Dream Mantras

A mantra is a short phrase, either spoken aloud or expressed in your mind, used as a meditation aid. Most people repeat their mantras in rhythm with their breathing. For years, I used this one:

- [While inhaling] "I am . . .
- [While exhaling] ". . . relaxed."

As part of your exploration of lucid dreams, you may wish to integrate dream mantras into your natural process of falling asleep. Once you're in bed, get comfortable, clear your mind, close your eyes, and try repeating one of the following dream mantras as you drift off. (Bear in mind most dream mantras are actually voiced "internally," not said aloud.) Align the mantra with your breath by repeating the first half as you inhale, and the second half as you exhale.

- I enjoy . . . lucid dreams.
- I know . . . when I'm dreaming.
- I control . . . my dreams.
- I am . . . a lucid dreamer.
- When the unexpected happens . . . I know I am dreaming.

As you fall asleep, your mantra streams inward, communicating directly with your subconscious mind. While you should feel free to come up with lucid dream-related mantras of your own, be sure your mantras are gentle and positive. As with affirmations, demanding mantras ("I must . . . have a lucid dream!") will quickly become more stressful than soothing.

Dream Meditations

Another way to set the stage for sleep is to use a dream meditation. Dream meditations are like dream visualizations generated during a meditative state.

To use a dream meditation, turn out the lights, stretch out in bed, and close your eyes. Follow your breathing, clearing your mind and narrowing your focus to the simple business of inhaling and exhaling.

When you notice your breath beginning to slow, meditate on the feeling of confidence and achievement you'll experience when you have a lucid dream. To make the meditation as effective as possible,

- DO focus on the emotion—what you'll feel;
- DO hold your emotional state for at least ten or twenty breath cycles;
- DO allow yourself, if you become sleepy, to drift off to sleep;
- DON'T try to create a detailed mental image of a dream;
- DON'T be hard on yourself if your attention wanders. Gently return to your focus;
- DON'T be surprised if you slip quickly and easily into a dream state.

The feeling of confidence and achievement generated by this meditation will follow you into your sleep.

New Sleeping Patterns

Having set the stage for healthy sleep, you can greatly improve your chances of achieving lucidity by making some minor—but highly effective—changes to your overall sleeping pattern.

Before you begin, take some time to map your current sleeping pattern by answering the following questions:

1. At what time of day do you usually wake up?

2. Most of the time, do you wake up naturally or with an alarm?

3. During the day, how frequently do you nap?

4. If you nap, about how long are your naps?

5. At what time of the day do you usually go to bed?

6. How many hours of sleep do you get per night?

7. How does your sleeping pattern differ on weekends or on "off days"?

Getting Healthy Sleep

We've noted again and again that seven to eight hours of sleep per night is the absolute minimum for healthy sleep. Sleep-starved individuals are not operating at their highest potential . . . and will very likely find it harder to achieve lucidity. By altering your sleep pattern to get more sleep, you increase your opportunities to experience a lucid dream.

Getting plenty of sleep is, for most people, a matter of priority. Just as we find time to do the things and see the people we really care about, we can, especially if lucid dreaming is a priority, find time to embrace a good night's sleep. If you're having difficulty making seven or eight hours of sleep per night fit your schedule, consider the following strategies:

1. Cut out an hour or two of television. If you have time to watch bad television, you have time in your schedule for better sleep. With an eye toward trimming back the time you spend in front of the squawk box, use the fast-forward feature on your Tivo, DVR, or VCR to speed past commercial breaks.

Consider limiting television to ninety minutes per night. In addition to giving you more time to sleep, limiting your television viewing time will quickly create a library of ready-to-watch shows (instead of leaving you with "nothing to watch" when television time rolls around).

2. Curtail social activity one hour earlier than normal. If lucid dreaming is a priority for you, you may want to cut back on late night activities with family and friends. Getting in the habit of ending your evening just one hour earlier than normal is an easy way to reclaim sixty precious minutes of sleep.

When friends tease you about becoming a recluse, just be honest with them. Tell them you're working on your ability to have lucid dreams . . . and that doing so requires plenty of sleep.

3. Time-shift at work. Given how quickly we eat these days, do you really need a lunch *hour*? Take a sandwich to the office (or eat at a nearby restaurant), reduce your lunch break to a half-hour, and ask your boss to let you come in a half-hour later (or to let you leave a half-hour earlier). In doing so, you'll reclaim thirty precious minutes you can devote to sleep.

4. Eat a light, quick dinner at home. In addition to improving the quality of your sleep by avoiding heavy dinners, a light, quick meal at home in the evening eliminates time spent getting to the restaurant, waiting for a table, ordering, waiting for your order, and getting back home again. A sandwich and bag salad or bowl of soup takes just twenty minutes to prepare and eat; a dinner out, by contrast, can easily eat up three hours of your evening!

5. Watch for opportunities to compress your daily schedule. Have a long commute from home to work? How long has it been since you explored moving closer to the office? If such a move is impossible, how might you pitch a "work from home" arrangement as a potential benefit to your employer?

Throughout your day, look for other ways to steal back minutes. Reduce travel time by completing all your errands in a single trip. Explore a ride-sharing arrangement that frees you from having to pick up the kids from school. Set yourself a time limit for checking email and surfing the web . . . and stick with it!

6. Burn less "midnight oil." Many night owls get into the habit of saving work (or putting off leisure) until late at night. At first, this makes sense: with most other people asleep, distractions are few and far between. Rather than give up sleep, explore strategies that limit interruptions without forcing you to stay up late.

When working, hang a "Do Not Disturb" tassel on the doorknob. Condition friends and family to expect you to be working during certain hours—and enforce those hours by refusing to answer telephone calls, email, or IMs during those hours. With a little self-management, you should be able to schedule plenty of time for work and sleep.

7. Perform a one-week schedule analysis. It's true: many people are overworked and under-rested. Especially if you work more than one job or have responsibility for kids, you may be one of them. Still, by performing a one-week analysis of your personal schedule, you may be able to reclaim as much as an hour of extra sleep time per day. Here's how:

Purchase a notepad small enough to carry with you everywhere you go. At least twice a day, pause long enough to jot down, in thirty-minute "chunks," how you've spent your time. (Don't use chunks smaller than thirty minutes. People who do so rarely complete this exercise.)

At the end of the week, review your notes. After a week of observation, you may discover that television is taking more time than you suspect, or you may notice a clear need to cut back other activities that quietly dominate your day.

Remember: every minute you can devote to healthy sleep is a minute you could be spending in a vibrant fantasy world of your own creation!

Napping

Sleep experts used to frown on daily naps, but this attitude is changing as we understand more about the nature of sleep. While long naps (of an hour or more) can disrupt your sleeping patterns, integrating a short nap into your schedule can refresh you . . . and improve your chances of experiencing a lucid dream.

You can get the most out of a nap by scheduling it to be taken, as often as possible, at a specific time of day. Many people find a fifteen-minute nap after lunch helps dispel the grogginess associated with having eaten a heavy meal;

others enjoy a mid-afternoon nap as a way of getting past that "late-in-the-day glaze" that makes them feel sluggish and worn down.

The key to effective napping? Timing. If a nap makes you feel drugged or thickheaded, you're napping long enough to slip down into the deeper stages of sleep. You can prevent this by setting a wristwatch or PDA alarm (or any other timer—even a simple alarm clock will do) to wake you in fifteen to twenty minutes.

You might also try the method mentioned earlier in this book: drifting off in a chair with a pen or pencil gripped between your forefinger and thumb. As you slip into sleep—a process that will take ten to fifteen minutes—your fingers will relax, causing you to drop the pen or pencil. Once it hits the floor, you'll wake up.

Best of all: nap time is prime time, as far as lucid dreaming is concerned. As you become accustomed to naps, you'll find it easier and easier to carry an image over from your waking thoughts into the dreamworld. And since you'll be waking very shortly, you're far more likely to recall your dreams—lucid or otherwise—when you wake up.

So, close that office door, turn off that cell phone, tell your kids to give you twenty minutes of peace … and encourage lucid dreaming by adding a quick nap to your daily routine.

Waking Early

When I first mention waking earlier than usual as a means of encouraging lucid dreams, people usually frown. "Wait a minute," they say. "You just spent the last half-hour badgering me to get more sleep. Now, you also want me to get up early! How can I possibly do both?"

When I talk about rising early as a method of inviting and encouraging lucid dreams, I'm not talking about getting up early. Instead, I'm proposing that you

- wake yourself an hour or ninety minutes earlier than usual,
- stay awake for fifteen minutes or so,
- go back to sleep and get up at your usual time.

Here's why: almost everyone who incorporates waking early into their sleep pattern reports having vivid, easily re-called dreams in their final hour of sleep. Even better, many lucid dreamers tell me they achieve lucidity more easily dur-ing these dreams than they do during any others.

I discovered this effect for myself, quite by accident. My partner, Clyde, is a dedicated early riser. Once Clyde's awake, he's up—he's just not the type to "laze around in bed," as Grandma used to say.

Generally, I require more sleep than Clyde, so I remain in bed for an additional thirty to forty-five minutes. Clyde's early departure wakes me, but ten to fifteen minutes later, I drift off to sleep again. The next half-hour or so is packed with vivid REM sleep. Upon waking, it's not unusual for me to recall two or three short, distinct dreams.

During my first lucid dreaming attempts, I also found it much easier to control the setting and content of these dreams. As I drifted off to sleep, I gently held the image of a place or person in my mind. Very frequently, that place became a dream destination and that person would appear before me in my dreams.

While this method is very effective for encouraging lucid dreams and enhancing dream recall, it's not for everyone. If you have difficulty waking and going back to sleep, or if you find that this process leaves you feeling groggy or tired, don't feel obligated to make early waking a part of your routine.

If you're curious about early waking as a shortcut to achieving lucidity, keep these tips in mind:

1. Work with the length of your waking time. Many lucid dreamers find that getting up early and staying awake for an hour or more (writing, recording dreams in a dream journal, answering letters, or watching television) before falling asleep again greatly enhances their ability to achieve lucidity. Others (like me) find that a shorter waking period works best. Try both, and see what works best for you.

2. Consider an alarm with two distinct alerts. Especially if you're headed to work shortly after waking, you don't want to condition yourself to sleep through your alarm! Buy an alarm clock with two alarm settings. Many will allow you to vary the alerts themselves—selecting a radio program for the first alarm and a buzzer for the second, for example. Over time, you can train yourself to wake just long enough to turn off the first alert and to "snap awake" when you hear the second.

3. Choose to snooze. Most alarm clocks incorporate a snooze feature, allowing the user to temporarily silence the alarm for a preset period of time. When time's up, the alarm goes off again. Some clocks allow you to set the length of your snoozing session. To encourage lucid dreaming, look for clocks that allow a snooze of at least thirty minutes.

4. Try a silent alarm. Your sleeping partner may not share your enthusiasm for waking early! If that's the case, you can still give the method a try by purchasing a silent alarm: a wristwatch that vibrates instead of sounding an audible alert. With a silent alarm in place, you can wake up early without waking your partner.

Gentle Waking

If waking early isn't appealing to you, you may wish to add one of my favorite alternatives to your personal sleeping pattern: gentle waking.

All my life, I've hated alarm clocks. Buzzers . . . bells . . . sirens . . . loud music: all of these alerts jolt me awake with such force, I'm dazed and jumpy for minutes afterward. In my opinion, an audio assault is a very bad way to start the day.

I also find that being "alarmed" first thing in the morning is not conducive to recalling my dreams. Because we experience our longest burst of REM sleep just before waking, it's not uncommon for an alarm to rouse us from a dream. For me, though, being jolted awake shatters the dream. When I use an alarm clock, I usually wake with dream fragments instead of detailed, comprehensive dream stories.

As a great alternative to those frightening beeps and buzzers, try alarm clocks that incorporate CD or MP3 players. In addition to playing a specific track at a specific time (I chose a recording of wind chimes and surf), many of these alarm clocks can be set to slowly and steadily increase speaker volume over several minutes. At the appointed time, the music or message you've chosen fades in very gently.

When I mention this option, some people always say, "Gentle surf? Wind chimes? Soft music? I'd never wake up!" Believe me: as the volume increases, you will.

An added benefit of this technique: frequently, your brain will incorporate the alert you've chosen into your dreams. When I was waking up to the sounds of surf, I often found myself dreaming of the beach. When I wake to a favorite song, I often notice it playing over a dream radio.

With time, I recognized the sound of surf or the sound of a favorite song as a dream cue—a sign that I was still asleep and dreaming. Since I had set my alarm clock to increase the volume very, very slowly over several minutes, I could recognize the dream cue, become lucid, and enjoy several minutes of lucidity before my alert became loud enough to wake me.

Since computers make it easier than ever to record and burn your own audio tracks, you might take this technology even further by using your own dream affirmations as an alert signal! Record your affirmations, burn a CD or convert them to an MP3, and load your alarm with the appropriate track. As the alarm fades in, your affirmations may well prompt you to realize you're dreaming!

If an audible alert—even one that fades in slowly—doesn't work for you, you might consider purchasing one of several alarm clocks that use light instead of sound. Alarms that incorporate flashing lights (or that flash lamps on and off) are fairly easy to find, but, especially with gentle waking in mind, you may prefer to purchase one of several "sunrise alarms" or "dawn simulators" that slowly shift from a subtle glow to an ever-brighter light.

Dream Tokens

Dream tokens—art, treasured objects, or deliberate arrangements of items with personal significance—are a creative, fulfilling way of inviting lucid dreams into your sleeping world.

Much has been made in recent years of the power of intention. Gurus of all stripes direct their followers not only to define what they want, but to represent that desire in some concrete way: by finding and framing a photo of the car they hope to purchase, for example. Feng shui, the art of harmonious placement, also encourages us to empower ourselves by placing meaningful objects—photographs, sculptures, fountains, lights—in positions associated with major life concerns.

As physical objects that represent your lucid dreaming goals, dream tokens fulfill a similar purpose. Like affirmations—audible reminders of your intention—dream tokens provide a visual reminder of your desire to achieve lucidity. Your personal dream token may be self-made or manufactured, personal or purchased. A dream token's power lies in its ability to reflect and remind you of your intentions, not in its origins.

In addition to prompting you to recall your lucid dreaming goals, dream tokens also serve as an announcement of those goals to the universe. Creating or selecting a dream token channels your intention into a physical form. Placing that dream token beside your bed is a deliberate action that reflects the seriousness of your intentions to achieve lucidity.

Your dream token may be a photograph, a beloved book, a special dream journal, a figurine, a crystal, or a flower. It may be a letter you write to yourself, to be opened when you experience your first lucid dream. It may be an object you associate with dreams and dreaming: a Native American dream catcher or a night-light.

Different people are drawn to different types of dream tokens; only you can know which dream token is right for you. When they hear about the dream token concept, many people know immediately what their dream token will be. Others invest a great deal of thought in the process. Some ideas you might consider include:

Collage art. When I mention collage as a means of producing a dream token, many people imagine spending hours and hours producing a poster-board-size work of art. If you're drawn to dramatic self-expression, there's certainly nothing wrong with a poster-sized collage. In terms of creating a dream token, though, a collage of any size—even one executed on a three-by-five index card—will be equally effective (and, perhaps, easier to keep at your bedside!).

For me, the appealing thing about using a collage as a dream token is the physical process of producing the art. First, there's the pleasure of searching for dream-like images in catalogs, magazines, and old postcards. Then, there's the satisfying work of cutting and trimming, followed by the experimental process of arranging your found elements on a sheet of cardboard.

Making a collage requires a fair degree of concentration and can become a meditation in itself. When the pieces are finally glued in place, you'll experience a feeling of achievement and satisfaction not always associated with dream tokens you could purchase in a store. You'll have created a one-of-a-kind piece that reflects your intentions and that is, above all, uniquely yours.

If your friends or family members are interested in lucid dreaming, a collaged dream token, designed with their goals in mind, can serve as a perfect, personal, handmade gift.

Treasured objects. Some people, given lots of time, plenty of magazines, sharp scissors, and several bottles of glue will produce little more than a great big mess. If collage just isn't for you, or if you lack the time to produce one, don't despair; you can use a treasured object as a dream token.

A treasured object is any item that holds special significance for you. It might be a plaque or award. It might be a stone you found at the beach. It might be the bright-yellow happy-face night-light that comforted you as a child. It might be a book your father read to you as part of a bedtime ritual. Family quilts, stuffed animals, scented candles—any or all of these, no matter what their monetary value, may be considered treasured objects.

Sandra keeps a small, plastic replica of the Eiffel Tower on her bedside table.

> All my life, I dreamed of going to Paris. For five years, I put money away. And then, the day finally came. I boarded the plane and spent two weeks just wandering the city. On the last day of my trip, I sat down on a sunny bench, stared up at the Eiffel Tower, and ate a chocolate croissant from a street vendor.
>
> I've never been happier. That trip showed me I can do anything, if I really put my mind to it. For me, this cheap little tourist trinket—I think I paid all of a dollar for it—brings back all the magic of my vacation in Paris. The minute I heard about dream tokens, I knew I could use the Eiffel Tower to make other dreams—including my lucid ones—come true.

A treasured object can be a powerful, nightly reminder of your intentions to dream a lucid dream. Sandra knew right away which object she wanted to use ... but if no particular object comes to mind, you have many other options, including the use of Tarot cards.

Tarot cards. Let's face it: Tarot cards aren't just for fortune-telling any more. In addition to being America's fastest-growing form of do-it-yourself therapy, Tarot cards are also being used as brainstorming tools, creative prompts, and powerful tools for envisioning and achieving personal goals.

With their evocative symbolic images and mythic themes, Tarot cards make perfect dream tokens. As you sort through the deck, look for cards that represent or resonate with your desire to have a lucid dream. In many decks, the Four of Swords (or its equivalent) depicts a sleeping or meditating person. You might also consider using the Fool (a card associated with new beginnings and creative leaps), the Magician (associated with "manifesting" intentions or making your dreams a reality), or the Moon (a trump card associated with sleep, dreams, romance, and fantasy).

After finding cards with images that evoke your intentions, create a small spread—or deliberate layout of cards—on your bedside table. You might, for example, pick one card to represent you, placing it in a position you call The Dreamer. Above The Dreamer's head, you might then place cards that reflect your efforts to have a lucid dream ... or even cards that depict people, places, activities, or themes you want to dream about.

There are literally thousands of decks on the market, and any of them will do just fine for the purpose of constructing a dream token. If the variety of available decks bewilders you, I encourage you to try any of the following decks, all of which possess a dream-like quality:

The World Spirit Tarot. This deck has bold colors, heavy lines, and stunning art. Its multicultural cast of characters will make it easy for you to find someone in the cards who looks like you! The deck's quasi-medieval setting includes fantastic characters galore.

Cosmic Tribe Tarot. Stevee Postman's amazing deck features dazzling artwork with images taken from both dreams and nightmares. Many cards from this deck depict the human body in all its naked glory, so if you're uptight about skin, it's not for you.

Gilded Tarot. Metallic surfaces, exquisite textures, and dreamy symbolism make this deck a perfect bedtime companion. As a mass-produced deck, it's affordable; if your budget allows, consider also getting the aptly named Tarot of Dreams by the same artist.

Any "Waite" deck, including the Universal Tarot. Pamela Colman Smith's haunting figures—found on every card of the Tarot created by Arthur E. Waite—have been redrawn and reinterpreted hundreds of times since they were first published around 1904. She's popular for a reason: in every scene, you get the impression that something important is just about to happen.

If you prefer something more contemporary, you might try *The Bright Idea Deck.* Restful, sleepy, and dream-like images can be found on several cards of this deck I developed especially for brainstorming use, including the Trump 2 (Intuition), Trump 18 (Optimism), Blue 9 (Satisfaction), Yellow 4 (Contemplation), and the Green suit's Comfort card.

Whatever deck you choose, select cards that reflect your intentions, place them by your bedside, and review them nightly as a means of reinforcing your desire to have a lucid dream. If Tarot cards aren't for you, you might consider runes, crystals, or any other magical objects for which you have an affinity.

Chapter 5 in a Nutshell

By employing just a few simple techniques, you can greatly increase your chances of enjoying a lucid dream.

Dream buddies—friends who share your desire for lucidity—can provide support, encouragement, and reinforcement. Affirmations, meditations, and visualizations can transform your frame of mind and focus your attention on your lucid dreaming goals. Small changes in your habits—including changes in how you prepare for and wake from sleep—can go a long way toward helping you achieve the lucid state. Finally, dream tokens—objects you pick out or create that represent your desire to have a lucid dream—can become powerful physical reminders of your quest for lucid dreams.

Adopting just one or two of these techniques can make a real difference in your lucid dreaming regimen. Try each one on for size, and feel free to adapt each technique to your special needs.

What's Next?

In chapter 6, "From Awareness to Lucidity," you'll find detailed introductions to two "lucid dreaming power tools"—the dream journal and reality checks. Enhancing your dream awareness with these tools will increase the frequency and stability of your dreams, providing you with more opportunities for achieving lucidity.

If you learn best from talking with people who have already mastered a skill, then feel free to skip to chapter 7,

"In Their Own Words." Here, you'll find interviews with lucid dreamers, along with tips and techniques you can put to work in your own lucid dreaming regimen.

In chapter 8, you'll find eleven lucid dreaming applications—experiments and experiences to try once you begin achieving lucidity on a regular basis.

Finally, in chapter 9, you'll find detailed information on how to interpret both traditional and lucid dreams. Using the simple methods outlined in this chapter, you'll have an easy time extracting meaning from the mysterious symbols you encounter in the dreamscape.

six

From Awareness to Lucidity

In this chapter, you'll discover:

- The benefit of dream journals, plus practical tips for getting the most out of monitoring and recording your dreams

- How making a habit of "reality checks" can vastly improve your dream awareness and recall

- Why achieving even tiny increases in dream awareness and control can make a dramatic difference in your quest for lucidity

Making Dreams a Priority

Inviting lucid dreams into your life—with dream buddies, affirmations, visualizations, healthier sleeping patterns, and dream tokens—can dramatically enhance your chances of having a lucid dream. Lucid dreams, though, don't have to be the sole focus of your effort. Lucid dreams are, after all, just one very special kind of dream. It follows quite logically that enhancing your awareness of dreams in general will also contribute to your pursuit of a lucid dream.

The heady pace of our waking world discourages a focus on dreams. We may wake with shreds of a story or fragments of a scene swirling in our heads. But the forward momentum of our day demands that we rise, shower, make breakfast, and streak out the door to work. By the time we take our first break, our dreams, like mist, have been burned away by the glare of the morning sun.

Things are only slightly better for those of us with curiosity about our dreams. We may ponder the meaning of a particularly vivid dream. We may be moved to tell others about a dream that struck us as strange, unusual, psychic, or prophetic. But in many cases, we, too, allow the vast majority of our dreams to return, unheeded, back into the darkness from which they came.

Becoming lucid dreamers involves a shift in both priority and focus. First, we must make recalling and exploring our dreams a priority. With the right tools and a little flexibility, this initial change is actually very easy to make. Second, we must also focus on our dreams—watching for patterns, scouring them for possible dream cues, and becoming aware of how our dreams tend to communicate with us. Ultimately, once we become aware of the dream state, we must slowly but surely achieve control of the world we experience there.

You can facilitate your own journey toward lucidity by keeping two things in mind:

- **The right tools make all the difference.** You're not alone in your efforts to achieve a lucid dream. Simple powerful tools exist that can have a huge impact on your ability to experience lucidity. In this chapter, we'll explore two remarkably simple, inexpensive, and powerful tools for enhancing dream awareness: dream journals and reality checks.

- **Control is a matter of degree.** You don't expect to rival Picasso the first time you lift a brush—so don't be surprised if your first taste of lucidity is brief, fleeting, or somehow incomplete. The information at the end of this chapter will help you make the most of small successes, transforming them into stepping-stones to more dramatic lucid dreaming achievements.

Two Simple Tools for Boosting Awareness
Power Tool # 1: The Dream Journal

In centuries past, the Ojibway, or Chippewa, tribe is believed to have instituted the practice of creating *dream catchers*— strands of sinew arranged into intricate webs, decorated with feathers or other sacred objects. Dream catchers, hung above an infant's bed, were believed to protect children, filtering out nightmares and allowing only the good dreams to pass through.

A dream journal is your personal twenty-first-century equivalent of a dream catcher. Unlike the Native American dream catcher, your dream journal is designed to capture *every dream* you have. Upon waking—even if it's in the middle of the night!—dedicated dream journalists flip open their dream journal and record every single dream and dream fragment they can recall. Take it from those of us who have adopted the practice: keeping a dream journal is the best and fastest way of building comprehensive dream awareness.

Dream Journal Techniques

The process is simple: when you wake up, you write down, as quickly as possible, any dreams you can remember. Make a separate entry for each dream. Be as descriptive as possible—the more you record, the more benefit you'll gain from this process.

These dreams might be fragmentary or full-scale epics. They may make sense, or they may be completely bewildering. You might remember the beginning and the end, but not how you got from A to B. Embrace this chaos as part and parcel of working closely with your dreams.

General Tips

- To keep a dream from fading while you write it, begin by outlining the dream, using a list of keywords to represent major events, objects, or people in your dream.

- Begin an entry by jotting down a few keywords or a thumbnail outline. This will help keep the dream fresh and help preserve fragments and transitions you would normally forget.

- After you record the dream—remember, the dream is most important, so it comes first!—be sure to record a title and date for each entry.

Using a Template. When it comes to dream journals, a little organization can go a long way. When you're groggy or sleepy, it can be difficult to remember exactly what you hoped to record! A template takes the guesswork out of dream journaling through a "fill in the blank" approach.

You don't need a fancy template with dozens of fields. In fact, you'll probably find that the following simple template will prompt you to recall the maximum number of details with the minimum amount of fuss:

Keywords/Quick Outline:

People:

Places:

Mood:

Dream Description:

Dream Title:

Date of Dream:

As noted previously, filling in the keywords and outline field first will help you preserve key features of the dream. The People/Places/Mood fields are also good places to jot down dream elements as they occur to you. (Take it from me: jot down dream elements as they occur to you. Almost every time you say, "Oh, yeah—I'll write that down in a minute!" you wind up forgetting that detail or why it seemed important at the time!)

The Dream Description field is the place to go wild, writing down everything you can recall as quickly as you recall it. Don't try to create reasoned, linear, publishable prose. Don't edit or rephrase. Your goal isn't to win a Pulitzer; your goal is to preserve as much of your dream on paper as possible. When you're done writing the description, give your dream a title (if you try to do this first, you'll waste valuable time debating potential titles!) and a date.

You can write these fields onto each page of your dream journal, or you can write them on the inside cover and refer to them as an outline as you make each entry.

Sample Dream Journal Entries

Dream journal entries don't have to be elaborate. Some people's dream journal entries read like novels ... but other people prefer to write brief summaries or capture their "stream of consciousness" following a dream experience.

The following examples provide an overview of the diversity of styles available to you. Feel free to experiment with these styles ... or to come up with a style that is uniquely your own.

Sample Entry #1

Keywords/Quick Outline: Turkey, pyramids, orange sky, scent of spices, water pots, tourists, translating, smoking, pipes

Dream Description: In this dream, I'm in a foreign city, somewhere in Turkey, I think, because of the odd keyhole-shaped doorways and minarets I can see on the horizon. In the middle of the city is a huge pyramid. Really, it's less than a pyramid and more like a ziggurat. It looks like the Tower of Babel does in old picture books: a tapering cone with a path coiled around it. Everyone is headed there for the festival, and so am I, even though I have no idea what the festival is.

The details of this dream amazed me. The sky is a vivid blend of orange and rose clouds; I think the sun is setting. As I walk with several friends—all of us wearing gold and purple robes—I can smell the food of the street vendors: cooking meat (chicken, I think) slathered with pungent spices. They are calling out to us in a foreign language. And that's a really odd detail: I know we're all speaking a foreign language, something other than English. Even so, I understand everyone perfectly.

At the tower, we are told to pick up several heavy water pots and carry them into a special festival room at the tower's base. I pick up one of the terra-cotta urns and struggle to get it inside, realizing, for the first time, just how hot it is here.

Inside the base of the tower are many tourists who have come for the festival. They are dressed in contemporary clothes: shorts and t-shirts and sundresses. They have cameras and are snapping photos of us constantly. I get the impression the occasion is meant to be somewhat solemn, but they are talking and laughing very loudly.

Because I know I also speak English, I go over to them and start explaining that this festival is meant to be an observation of silence. They are very apologetic, but they also have many questions. Eventually, I am able to translate their questions for my people, and then translate their answers back into English. I enjoy the facility with which I can switch between the two languages, and I feel very important during this part of the dream.

Eventually, they catch on to the spirit of the event and settle down on huge pillows. A series of women bring out water pipes and some dried herbs, and all of us pass the pipes, which make a hollow, watery noise when we draw on them. The smoke is sweet and smells like basil.

I am thinking of food—what kind I should order for the tourists—when I wake up, feeling very confused about where I am. For several minutes after the dream, I feel displaced, as though I've been uprooted from where I belong and plopped down here in someone else's very mundane reality.

Dream Title: Working as a Translator

Dream Date: June 15

Sample Entry #2

Keywords/Quick Outline: ducks, burlap bag, feed, alligators, big stick, kids laughing

Dream Description: I'm by a lake. There are a lot of yellow ducks. I want to feed them, but I don't have any bread. In the grass, I find a big bag, like a bag of fertilizer. Inside, it's full of bright green seed. I toss the seed to the ducks. They get together in a big group, quacking and fighting.

All of a sudden, a big alligator comes out of the water and snaps up several ducks. He comes out again and again. I try to shoo the ducks away, but they won't leave because of the feed. I feel very guilty, so I get a big stick and start hitting the alligator on the snout. I hit him over and over again, but he won't quit eating ducks.

A group of kids walks by, and I holler at them for help. They think what I'm doing looks funny, and all they do is point and laugh.

Dream Title: Dead Ducks

Dream Date: January 2 (afternoon nap)

Sample Entry #3

Keywords/Quick Outline: stacks, piles, tiles, Thailand, Andy Dick

Dream Description: Thailand, hot shack, hot even in the shade under the tin roof. Dusty factory makes fragile bathroom floor tiles. My job—organize mountains of random tiles into stacks according to color and price. Every time I get the stacks done, about a million more tiles come out of the chute. Many hit the floor and break. This is considered my fault.

My supervisor is comedian Andy Dick: red-faced, angry, sweaty, steamy glasses, always unhappy. "I could have done this hours ago! You should be finished! No one else breaks this many tiles!" He hovers over me constantly. Whatever I do, even if it's something I do because he said to, he screams that I should be doing something else. "Wash those first! How can you tell what color it is if you don't wash it! Now what are you doing? You have to clear the broken tiles before you wash the others, or you can't tell the garbage from the final product! Now what are you doing? Didn't you say you had experience doing this?"

I don't have experience doing this. As soon as I realize that, I wake up.

Dream Title: Sorting Piles

Dream Date: March 3

* * * * *

As you can see, the entries above differ greatly in tone and the amount of detail. There's no right or wrong way to do an entry . . . and every person's dream journal will be very different. Rather than try to do it right . . . just do it! Record events, feelings, images, objects, people—anything and everything that comes to mind.

Benefits of Keeping a Dream Journal

Dream more dreams. Keeping a dream journal requires a little self-discipline, but that discipline pays off! As you keep your commitment to record your daily dreams, you are sending a strong, silent message to your subconscious mind that remembering your dreams is very important to you. This daily focus on dreams and dreaming quite naturally conditions you to have more vivid dreams more frequently.

Recall dreams in greater detail. At first, you may find you recall only one or two dreams (or dream fragments) per night. Don't hesitate to record fragments or little bits and pieces that don't seem connected to a larger dream. Writing down one detail will often bring other details to mind, and the process of recording a dream fragment frequently helps you recapture the larger dream from which the fragment came.

In addition, as you record the details of one dream, other dreams may come back to you. Many dream journalists deliberately recall their dreams in reverse order, working backward from a dream they had just before waking to dreams they had earlier in the night.

Remember more dreams. After keeping a dream journal for two months, I went back to read earlier entries. As I read over my dream activity for the past sixty days, I was stunned. While I remembered many of the dreams in my journal, *about one-third of the dreams I had recorded had faded entirely from my memory!*

In some cases, reading a journal entry about a dream would prompt me to remember it. There were several entries, though, that seemed to have come from someone else's dream journal. I knew that, at some point, I had written those dreams down ... but the dream experience had faded so completely, I could not recall having dreamed those dreams at all.

The experience convinced me that all of us dream far more than we realize. With this in mind, your dream journal can become a permanent storage space for your dreams. Even after your dreams fade from your memory, they can be accessed quickly and easily from the journal.

Discover dream cues. After reviewing two or three months of entries from my dream journal, I discovered several elements in my dreams that I'd never noticed before:

- *Elevators.* About one in five dreams involved elevators. In every case, the elevator had some remarkable feature. One incorporated a floor selector with thousands of buttons. Another was the size of a small theatre, capable of ferrying hundreds of people at once. Pretty often, the elevators in my dreams get stuck, fall, or otherwise malfunction.

- *Celebrities.* Up front: I'm not starstruck at all. I couldn't care less about celebrity news, and I would be hard pressed to name a favorite movie star or television actor. How odd, then, to discover how often celebrities appear in my dreams! Often, they seem to be "extras" my subconscious uses to flesh out the dreamworld: Val Kilmer will be a postman, or Katie Holmes will show up as a boarder at my mother's house, or Tom Hanks, pad in hand, will show up as a waiter.

- *Unusual damage.* Before my eyes, a crater will form in the floor of a parking garage, revealing a pool of bright-green goo. Struck by a heavy object, a pane of glass will shatter, creating a web of cracks that spell out a word. Sturdy objects—metal doors, buildings, trees—fall apart with the slightest tap.

These and other motifs occur again and again, but, until I kept a dream journal, I had no idea how often these images appeared in my dreamworld. Now that I know about these repeating elements, I use them as dream cues. When George Clooney appears to apologize for the rusted-out floor of an elevator the size of a small house, I now realize: "Hey! I'm dreaming!" and take control of the world.

Things to Consider when Selecting Your Dream Journal

Off-the-Shelf Appeal. Is a commercial dream journal for you? Dream journals have become so popular, many bookstores carry blank books created especially for this purpose.

These usually consist of blank pages bound with fanciful covers in every possible magical hue: pale pink, lavender, rich purple, metallic gold. Commercial dream journals usually feature decorative prints or finishes that suggest dreams and dreaming: shooting stars, crescent moons, countable sheep. If you find these journals appealing, or if you see purchasing one of these as a way of expressing your intention to become more aware of your dreams, then by all means, pick one up.

That said, almost any pad or notebook of any kind can work well as a dream journal, so don't feel you have to invest in a manufactured one. As long as you keep your journal faithfully, your dream journal will do its work. A simple fifty-cent notepad can work just as well as that $12.50 lavender silk-bound tome with glitter-dusted stars!

Size Matters. What size should your dream journal be? That's easy: a dream journal should always be exactly 5.5 inches wide and 8.5 inches tall.

Just joking! While that sort of dogmatic prescription would certainly make picking out a dream journal easier, it's much more practical to allow your personal sleeping habits and bedroom environment to determine the size of journal that works best for you.

Notepads. Those simple, pocket-sized pads with a spiral coil of wire across the top make fine dream journals. A notepad slips easily in a pocket or purse, making it extremely portable. If you nap during the day or doze on the train ride home, notepad dream journals can always be close at hand. If you travel often, their compact size makes them easy to pack.

Especially if you tend to recall your dreams in fragments, a notepad can be a perfect choice, as you can dedicate a single page to each dream and fill it with the images and ideas you recall. On the other hand, if you tend to remember your dreams in great detail, you may find breaking your dream over several pages feels awkward ... or that your notepads fill up too quickly.

Pocket journals/Moleskine journals. Pocket journals come in a variety of sizes. Most are larger than notepads, giving you plenty of room to record your observations. They also come in a variety of formats and colors. My first dream journal was kept in a thin, palm-sized blank book with an elastic band, sold in bookstores as a Moleskine journal. The size was perfect for stowing under a pillow or positioning on the bedside table, and the elastic band did double duty, marking the next available blank page and keeping the book closed while traveling.

Be sure to pick out a familiar or well-established brand of pocket journal, especially if you choose the refillable type with a reusable cover. You don't want to get attached to a particular type of journal ... only to discover a few weeks down the road that refills are no longer available!

Letter or legal pads. These give you ample space for recording your dreams. Because you can find these pads at any office supply or general-interest store, you will never lose time to a desperate search for refills.

A letter or legal pad, especially when bound in a leather or plastic folder, may be too big or ungainly to be easily portable. If you go this route, make sure you've got plenty of room for it on your bedside table. Will carrying around a pad of this size feel awkward or uncomfortable? If so, pick something smaller and lighter.

Binding Agreements. Spiral- or wire-coil-bound notebooks are light and inexpensive. If budget is a concern, a spiral-bound notebook is very likely your best choice.

Be aware, though, of two major disadvantages of spiral-bound notebooks. First, as you tear pages out, you'll create numerous strips of waste paper. Since your dream journal may well be used in bed, you might want to consider whether or not you want these sharp curls of paper between your sheets! Second, the wire coils of spiral-bound notebooks don't hold up well over time. If you plan to use your dream journal for several months (or to store a series of them), a spiral-bound notebook may not be your best choice.

Small pocket journals are usually bound by two staples or a strip of glue; like spiral-bound journals, these may not endure much wear and tear. Midsized and large pocket journals tend to be glue-bound with cardstock, cardboard, vinyl, or leather covers. These are both flexible and durable; they make great choices for dream journals.

Three-hole binders offer the ability to add and remove pages on the fly. Those designed to use standard notebook paper, however, may prove too large. The tiny clasps in smaller versions often become bent or misaligned, ruining the entire notebook.

Keep in mind, too, that punched-hole paper tears easily away from the metal clasps. Should you accidentally yank out a valuable dream entry, reinserting the lost page can be difficult or impossible.

The Paper Chase. Unlined paper gives you the most flexibility, allowing you to fill pages with free-form text, drawings, and sketches. Especially if you have neat handwriting, unlined paper may be your best choice.

Lined paper helps keep your pocket journal looking neater. If you prefer lined paper, remember that you may often be using the journal in low-light conditions in a darkened room. With this in mind, choose paper with dark, bold lines.

You may also find pads, pocket journals, and notebooks featuring graphing paper. If keeping your text a uniform size (for legibility) is important to you, if you like to create precisely indented outlines, or if you plan to sketch some things you dream about, this may be your best choice.

Any well-stocked office supply store will carry notepads, pocket journals, notebooks, and pads in all three paper styles.

True Colors. Many of the commercially prepared dream journals come with colored paper: pastels, pinks, and purples. These can look very pretty, and, if you enjoy colored paper, you may want to use these.

As mentioned in the previous section, though, your dream journal will very likely be used in low-light conditions. Deep-purple paper may look pretty, but reading black or blue print on purple paper in a darkened bedroom can be very difficult and frustrating! I know one woman who chose a dream journal with pink pages . . . only to discover later that her entries (written with a red pen) became virtually illegible as her journal aged.

The greater the color contrast between your pen and paper, the more legible your dream journal will be. With long-term readability in mind, I recommend black ink on crisp, white paper.

Other Features. As a general rule, the more basic your dream journal, the better. Dangling ornaments, large and clumsy bookmarks, mirror tile glued to the cover, and other enhancements may look good at first. Unfortunately, they also tend to break, get lost, or pull away, making your dream journal look worn and dirty.

Some good features to look for include the following:

- *Pockets.* If a page pulls away from the binding, you can always file the dream away in a pocket. A pocket is the perfect place to carry pictures, Tarot cards, or other images you use as dream catalysts.

- *Pen loops.* Dreams fade quickly. In the time it takes to retrieve your journal and scrabble around the bedroom for a pen, the details of your first foray into lucidity can slip away. A pen loop—a simple band of plastic, cloth, or leather on the inside or spine of your journal just large enough to slip a pen or pencil into—increases the likelihood that you'll always have a pen around when you need one!

- *Template pages.* Some people prefer free-form dream journaling: whatever occurs to them, they write down. Others—especially people who tend to be groggy upon waking—find template pages (preprinted outlines with blanks you can fill in) to be very useful. You can duplicate the template provided earlier in this chapter or create your own.

OTHER HELPFUL TOOLS

Pens. A good pen is your dream journal's best friend. For dream journaling, I think pens are better than pencils. Pencil print becomes increasingly smeary and faded with age. Because pencils allow you to erase, you'll be tempted to spend time editing instead of recording. Pens also tend to be more comfortable to use when writing rapidly.

Frankly? Rather than splurge on a decorated notebook (you can always decorate your own!), I advise people to splurge on a dream pen! A pen you received as a gift, a pen you buy to commemorate a special achievement, a pen with an interesting shape or color—all of these make great dream pens.

A number of pens now on the market come with bright white lights embedded in the barrel—perfect for jotting down journal entries in the dark!

Lights. For just a moment, imagine yourself having a particularly vivid and enjoyable lucid dream. You wake up in the middle of the night, excited and fulfilled. "I've got to write this down!" you think, and you roll to the side of the bed, reach for your dream journal, and switch on the lamp.

Ouch! When you've just spent several hours in total darkness, the glare of your bedside lamp is likely to be painful. (If you share your bed with someone, he or she is also likely to disapprove of your use of a bright light at 2:30 in the morning!) As you sit there blinking and grinding your fists into your eyes, precious dream details are fading away.

If you can afford nothing else, a bedside lamp will do. There are a few alternatives, though, and most of these can be picked up—either new or on eBay—at very little expense:

- *Pens with lighted barrels.* As just mentioned, these are perfect dream journal pens. Go for one with a bright white LED. Avoid colors, which conceal more than they reveal.

- *Book lights.* There are dozens of brands available, and all are variations on one theme: a miniature gooseneck lamp you can clip to the top of your notebook. Some are brighter and more durable than others, so shop at stores that let you try them out before buying, or purchase yours from a store with a generous return policy.

- *Headlamps.* Sold in camping and sports stores, headlamps are lightweight headbands with a bulb and reflector attached. Center the mini-light on your forehead, slip on the headband, and you're good to go! These battery-powered lights put out a cone of extremely focused, very bright white light . . . but because the light is directed away from you, the glare isn't a problem.

ALTERNATIVES TO NOTEBOOKS

In *The Artist's Way*, author Julia Cameron urges her readers to keep a daily "morning pages" journal. Cameron, who believes that "writing things rights things," strongly advises her students to write these journals by hand.

Over the years, I've met a number of people who simply aren't comfortable writing by hand. For them, pens feel awkward and using them gives rise to hand cramps and sore fingertips. If writing by hand isn't your thing (or if you discover that your late-night handwriting is often illegible), you might consider one of these alternatives:

PDAs. Personal digital assistants, or handheld computers, may, at first, seem like the perfect choice for fatigue-free dream journaling. They're lightweight, and most have lighted screens (perfect for making entries in the dark!). Transferring your dream journal to your desktop computer is as simple as dropping the device in its recharging cradle.

On the other hand, most PDAs incorporate some kind of (frequently unreliable) handwriting recognition software; unless you're proficient with this kind of data entry (or unless you use one of the few PDAs with a keyboard), you may want to avoid using a PDA.

Laptop computers. I love a good laptop, and eventually I began typing my early-morning dream journal entries into the same computer I used to write this book. As long as I went straight to the computer first thing in the morning, this worked well ... but I confess I often lost late-night dreams because I told myself, "I'll just go type this up tomorrow morning."

If you use a laptop, keep it powered up at all times (while you wait for it to boot up or wake from hibernation, dreams are fading!). Be aware, too, that a keyboard makes for noisy entries. If you share a bed with someone else, he or she might not appreciate the clackety-clack of keys in the dead of night.

Voice recorders. A voice-activated recorder (or even an iPod or other MP3 player with a microphone attachment) is one of the better alternatives to pen and paper. Once you become familiar with the controls, you can make your journal entries without turning on a single light, and you can always transcribe your recordings later.

If you work with a recorder, bear in mind that your late-night voice is lower and thicker than your daytime voice. Make a special effort to speak clearly, or you may wind up recording little more than slurred speech. Keep fresh cassettes handy, or be sure to off-load digital content on a regular basis; you don't want to lose a dream because you ran out of tape or memory!

A Word about Confidentiality

Your dream journal entries are deeply personal. Your dreams shed light on everything from your greatest hopes to your darkest fears. It's probably not a good idea to keep the dream journal where just anyone can get to it, especially if you record details that are disturbing, sexual, or highly personal. I recommend you keep your dream journal stored in a safe place during the day to avoid having someone stumble upon it.

If you choose to keep your dream journal on a computer or handheld device, I strongly recommend you use passwords or encryption software to secure your dreams from prying eyes.

Power Tool #2: Performing Reality Checks

Remember the definition of lucid dreaming we established at the beginning of this book?

Put simply, lucid dreams are dreams in which the dreamer

- becomes aware that he or she is dreaming, and
- achieves a degree of control over the content and direction of the dream.

For most of us, the trickiest part—the critical first step—is becoming aware that we're dreaming.

The dreamworld looks and feels real. In addition, dreams suppress our critical faculties, making us less likely to object when impossible situations occur. In the waking world, if we were confronted with a man who changed into a minotaur and began to offer us tips on dancing the tango, we would likely balk. When dreaming, though, we take such transformations and illogical juxtapositions in stride.

That presents a big challenge for lucid dreamers, whose ability to "wake up" to the fact they're having a dream is usually tied to noticing an objectionable detail—strange transformations, impossible abilities, clocks without hands, or books without print, for example. The answer? Reality checks. Reality checks are habitual pauses during which you ask, "Am I dreaming? Is this a dream?"

TYPES OF REALITY CHECKS

You begin by incorporating reality checks into your waking-world routine. Some simple methods for doing so include:

Threshold checks. Every time you pass through a doorway, condition yourself to wonder whether you're dreaming or awake. Scan the room around you for dream cues: furniture that's out of place, unfamiliar objects, people who behave in abnormal ways. (If you live in a college dorm, of course, these things may be a part of your everyday environment!)

Time checks. Whenever you check your watch or see a clock, ask yourself, "Is this a dream?" Take advantage of the fact that timepieces behave irrationally in dreams! Check every clock you see two or three times. Can you read the face of the timepiece clearly? Does time appear stable? Do the numbers you're seeing make sense?

Storage checks. When you place something in your pocket or purse, pause to ask, "Am I dreaming?" Once the object is in place, pat your pocket or glance inside your purse. Is it still there? Has it changed? Are there other objects in your pocket or purse that seem unusual or out of place? If you retrieve the object, does it behave as you would expect it to?

Text checks. When you see a newspaper, study the front page carefully. Is the content stable? Do pictures or headlines change when you read them multiple times? Is the text unusually difficult to read? If you look away and look back, do you see any changes? You can perform the same sort of test on books and other printed material.

Random checks. Purchase an inexpensive wristwatch with an alarm or stopwatch feature. Throughout the day, set the alarm to random times, or set the stopwatch to count down a random number of hours and minutes. Whenever your wrist alarm or stopwatch beeps, ask yourself, "Is this a dream?"

Dream cue checks. Once you've kept a dream journal for several weeks, you'll begin to notice patterns—repeating motifs and recurring events—that are sure signs that a dream is in progress. Because I know towers, elevators, and celebrities are personal dream cues, I perform reality checks whenever I see a cell phone tower, enter an elevator, or spy someone who looks like a celebrity. (Good thing I don't live in Los Angeles, I guess.)

If you're clever, you've already figured out why reality checking can be such a powerful tool for lucid dreamers. How many times a day do you walk through a door? How often do you check the time? How often do you stow something in a purse or pocket? Even if you adopt only one of these events as your personal "reality check trigger," you'll find yourself performing simple reality checks several times a day.

The result? Over time, reality checks become a habit— an integral part of your personal routine. As such, they carry over from the waking world into the dreamworld.

Before long, as you cross a dream threshold, check a dream wristwatch, or jam a dream Kleenex into your dream purse, you'll ask, entirely by reflex, "Is this a dream?"

And it will be!

DON'T "BOUNCE" YOUR REALITY CHECKS!

A final note about reality checks: when you perform them, be suspicious of the first answer that occurs to you. If you build a habit of automatically answering, "No, this is reality," that habit, too, will carry over into the dreamworld. What good are reality checks if, each time you check your reality, you habitually dismiss the possibility that you're dreaming?

Two simple strategies can help you avoid this potential pitfall:

1. **As part of determining which world you're in, try something simple ... but impossible.** I've chosen floating—a behavior I can't seem to master in the real world, but which comes very naturally to my dream self—as my standard test. When I ask, "Is this a dream?" I will myself to levitate a few inches off the floor. In the real world, gravity pins me down. In dreams, I almost always drift skyward.

If floating isn't your thing (or if your years of studying yoga and meditation have given you the ability to levitate in the waking world!), pick another subtle, impossible behavior. Friends of mine attempt to summon dead relatives, change the color of the walls, or change day to night. If old Aunt Sarah (God rest her soul) comes walking in, if the room goes from beige to hot pink, or if the blue sky is suddenly replaced by a dark one, they know to assume control and start enjoying themselves.

Choose these impossible events with care! In dreams, I often lose teeth in a variety of bizarre ways: cracking them, chipping them, shattering them. Since I've always had healthy teeth, it seemed quite reasonable to use "loss of teeth" as a dream cue. The next time my teeth slid out of my mouth (joined together, oddly enough, by a little chain, as though my teeth were a strand of pearls), I realized I was dreaming. Success!

Not long after, during a meal in the waking world, I cracked a crown. Even as my mouth filled with sharp shards and gritty fragments, I thought, "I'm dreaming!"

I wasn't—but for several minutes, the feeling that I *might* be dreaming was inescapable and unsettling.

Whatever you do, don't pinch yourself. While folk wisdom teaches us to say, "Pinch me! I must be dreaming," dream researchers note that dream pinches hurt just as much as their real-world counterparts.[1] As such, they're lousy reality checks!

2. Throw in a few "false positives." When you first adopt reality checks, you'll very often (and very quickly) establish the fact that you're not dreaming. As mentioned earlier, if you're not careful, you'll condition yourself to always answer the question "Am I dreaming?" with a definite and self-defeating "Nope!"

---

1 Stephen LaBerge and Howard Rheingold, *Exploring the World of Lucid Dreaming* (New York: Ballentine Books, 1990), 63.

Mix things up with a false positive—a deliberate wrong answer. Occasionally, even when a reality check proves you're awake, reach the conclusion, "Yes! I'm dreaming!" Feel elated. Congratulate yourself on having achieved consciousness within a dream. Pause a few seconds and picture yourself, as vividly as possible, taking control of your reality and altering it to suit your personal tastes.

If you incorporate false positives into your routine, they'll follow you into your dreams. At some point, even as the dreamworld's characteristic critical suppression tricks you into saying, "No, I'm not dreaming," you'll throw out a "false" positive . . . and shock yourself by very casually assuming control of what turns out to be a dream after all!

Making a habit of questioning reality can, at first, seem a little unsettling. At first, you may feel silly or self-conscious when doing so. That said, if you can get into the habit of performing reality checks on a regular basis, you'll be taking a major step toward achieving lucidity in your dreams.

Achieving Control

Once you manage to become more aware of your dreams (and the dream state in general), you'll confront your next challenge: moving from awareness to control. Some people make this shift easily. Others achieve the transition only after investing a great deal of time and practice. Elizabeth wrote to me about her own frustration with the process:

> After keeping the dream journal for three weeks, I began
> to have more dreams and remember them better. Then
> I started reality checking. Four nights later, I spotted my

prompt (Percy, my cat) in a dream. When I bent down to pet him, I asked, "Am I dreaming?"

While I hadn't noticed it until that moment, right away I knew I was dreaming. The room around me wasn't as distinct as it is when I'm awake, and there was something wrong with the way the pictures were hung on the walls. (They were floating about a quarter inch off the wall, without nails or wires to hold them in place.)

It hit me like lightning! "I'm dreaming!" But I got so excited, I woke up right away.

Over the next two weeks, this happened over and over again. I did my reality check, discovered I was dreaming, and woke myself up.

Elizabeth's experience is quite common. When the elation of awareness grips us, many of us are so happy and excited, we jolt ourselves awake. Fortunately, with practice, you can get past the shock of finding yourself in a lucid dream. With time, the novelty of consciousness will give way to a feeling of confidence and a sense of direction.

Plan for Lucidity

It helps to have a plan. In the real world, we recognize the value of planning for the unexpected. With an eye toward a possible accident, we take out insurance. With the potential for disaster in mind, we dutifully file out of our office buildings for a fire drill. We do this for a good reason: in the waking world, people who have a plan—those who made arrangements to pay their bills or who know the location of the nearest fire escape—perform better than those who don't.

The same holds true for the dreamworld. Right now, in the waking world, you should invest a few minutes planning what you'll do when you do achieve lucidity. Once you realize you're in a dream, what will you do? Will you try to fly? Will you summon a high school sweetheart you haven't seen in decades? Will you visit the set of your favorite television show? Will you visit Paris?

Plan your first lucid dream outing in advance. Envision it. Imagine it. Experience it in a detailed visualization or daydream. If you do so, when you achieve awareness ("I'm dreaming!"), you're far less likely to respond with shock . . . and far more likely to shift your attention to the business of making your dreams come true.

Creeping toward Control

Many lucid dreamers expect the assumption of control to be an all-or-nothing process. In my own experience, people rarely jump from helplessness to total control. For most of us, the assumption of control is a gradual process. As we practice, we achieve control more often . . . and, ultimately, we achieve a finer degree of control.

Several people I interviewed talked about this process. Terri wrote, "Aaarrgh! I'm so frustrated! I see a cue, I get that I'm dreaming, and I go for it. At first, things are cool. I can clear the room. I can fade to white. But after that, I'm just stuck in this white space. I try and try to manifest the garden I want to see, but it's useless. After a while, I just give up and wake up.

Brent enjoyed more success, but still felt frustrated. "Maybe I get in too much of a hurry, or something. Like last week. I knew I was dreaming, because the view out of my apartment window was wrong. So before I could wake up, I focused on seeing Dale. And I could see him. But something was wrong. Even though he was right there, he seemed very far away, or maybe transparent. I wound up dreaming about talking to Dale—like you might imagine just talking to someone, without knowing the details—instead of actually having a conversation with him. It felt fake."

Even Jay, who regularly enjoys lucid dreams, admitted, "About one out of three times, I'm not getting what I want. I'll change one of the dream people into Juanita, but she'll change into someone else, and I can't fix it. Or I'll manage to see the pyramids, but they'll be more like cardboard cutouts, or they'll look like they've been printed onto big sheets of vinyl. Pretty often, I'll get control, but then forget I'm lucid, and just start going with the flow, even when I don't mean to."

My own early lucid dreams were characterized by less-than-perfect control. Here's a dream-journal entry I wrote the morning after achieving my first lucid dream:

Success! I successfully produced my first lucid dream last night. In the dream, I walked into an elevator with an odd feature: hundreds and hundreds of buttons lining the walls. At first, a standard dream reflex kicked in: "That's odd," I said, and I prepared to move on.

Then it hit me: I'm in an elevator. Something strange is going on. I did my reality check and saw that the labels on the elevator buttons weren't consistent. Then it hit me: *I'm dreaming.*

Immediately, I willed the elevator doors to open on a bright, sunlit meadow; they did. Once in the meadow, I thought of several people I wanted to see: a college friend, a friend who's moved away, and a television character. As soon as I thought of them, these people appeared.

At this point, I was afraid I would wake up and lose the dream, so I rushed up to speak with them. Unfortunately—maybe because I'm a beginner at this?—they weren't quite themselves. They felt real (I hugged one), and they looked real, but they were like bodies without brains. The trio staggered around the meadow, slack-jawed as zombies. No matter how hard I tried to make them behave normally, they just stumbled around and bumped into each other.

Since that first dream, I've faced this challenge again and again: the people I summon in dreams are "zombies" about 50 percent of the time. They look right. They feel right. They're dressed (or undressed!) exactly as I would expect. Even so, they're strangely devoid of emotion or life; it's as though they're drugged or drunk.

If control escapes you, or if you're not assuming the degree of control you hoped, keep the following things in mind:

Start small. When learning to paint, you wouldn't expect to produce a masterpiece on Day One. When pursuing lucidity, don't expect to generate an entire world during your first lucid dream!

Set small, conservative initial goals. Float. Fly. Summon someone who looks like an old friend. Change one tiny aspect of your surroundings: the weather, the quality of the light, the music playing on your iPod. Once you can implement these subtle changes, take on more challenging goals.

Celebrate steps toward success. At one point, I received this email from a young woman who was just beginning to have lucid dreams again after years of not having them. "I want to speak to my mother. I can get back to my old house. I can smell dinner in the kitchen. I can even get her in the room. She's never facing me, and she won't speak to me. I feel like a total failure!"

My young friend's obsession with one goal—speaking to her mother in a dream—was blinding her to her incredible success. Rather than celebrate her ability to generate an environment, summon the fragrance of a well-prepared meal, and have her mother actually appear in the dream, she focused on her failure to make her dream mother turn to her and speak!

Incomplete control beats no control at all! As you pursue lucidity, celebrate every small step toward the assumption of control (even if you take the same small step over and over again!) as a complete and total victory.

Consider switching goals. If one goal eludes you over a long period of time, perhaps it's time to change your target. Rather than doggedly pursuing a date with your perfect mate, perhaps you should try visiting a foreign port, changing the color of the sky, or meeting with another friend or family member for a pleasant visit.

Interestingly, I know at least two people who achieved their original dream goals only after giving up on them! Here's what Kelly, who wanted one more fishing trip with her grandfather, had to say:

> So I eventually just quit trying to get back to that morning and started going to the woods instead. Over the next week, I was able to make a forest, complete with towering redwoods and mossy boulders, several times.
>
> One of those times, while concentrating on filling the trees with birds, I stumbled on a lake. I realized this was the lake PopPop used to carry me to. Then, there he was, out on the lake, smiling and waving. I somehow managed to get into the boat, and he handed me a pole.

Remember to relax. Lucid dreaming is not a life or death priority. Relax! You're dreaming, not curing cancer. If the pursuit of lucidity starts to disrupt the quality of your sleep, or if you find yourself frustrated by a lack of control, take a break. No one's going to grade your progress, and this isn't a competition. Take a deep breath, get some perspective, and try again in a few days.

Techniques for Maintaining Dream Control

Once you achieve a degree of control over your dreams, you'll face two new challenges: maintaining lucidity and extending the duration of your lucid dreams.

Maintaining lucidity is a matter of retaining your awareness that you're in control of the dreamworld. Because you tend to become very much involved in whatever you're experiencing, it's easy to become distracted, forget that you're in charge, and slip back into an unconscious state.

Many lucid dreamers also report that, in their excitement over having created a lucid dream, they shift from experiencing the dream to having a conversation about it. Anita noted:

> After a few minutes of being lucid, I wind up sitting in the kitchen, talking to my roommate about what went on in my lucid dream. At that point, I have no idea that I'm still dreaming. When strange things start happening, I ignore them. But when I wake up, I realize that I was lucid at first and then not lucid later on. It makes me so angry!

Those who eventually maintain lucidity throughout their dream may also have to struggle to stay in the dream realm. "Just when things get good," Kristin told me, "I start waking up. And I can actually *feel* myself waking up! It's like the dream room gets darker, and the person I'm with and the bed start fading out, and I get all confused. If I strain, I can sometimes get back. If I go right back to sleep, I can usually get back. But it's like my dreams don't want me to be lucid. The whole time I'm dreaming, something's trying to wake me up!"

As you become a more proficient lucid dreamer, there are at least three strategies you can employ to stabilize and extend your lucid state.

Spinning

Lucid dreaming literature is peppered with accounts of people who use spinning—physically twirling their dream bodies around and around in tight circles—as a means of stabilizing and extending their dream states.

This comes as no surprise to many lucid dreamers I've spoken with, many of whom seem to have hit on this strategy without having come across it in books or articles. "I thought I was the only one," Kim said. "It sounds crazy, in fact. But if I feel myself waking up, I kneel down like some kind of Russian folk dancer, stick out one leg, put all my weight on the other, and spin, spin, spin. The dream may change around me, but I stay asleep, and I stay in control. After, I can get up and get back to whatever I was doing."

While I lack Kim's dream dancing ability, I've also adopted spinning as a means of prolonging a dream and preserving lucidity. Perhaps the physical nature of spinning forces your dream self to be more centered in your dream body. Perhaps the act of watching the world spin around you forces your eyes to track from side to side, reinforcing the physical response associated with REM sleep. In the end, I don't have a clue why spinning works . . . but it does work.

Other lucid dreamers tell me that other repetitive physical actions work just as well, including jumping, hopping, clapping, flailing their arms, and stamping their feet.

ANCHORING

One clever lucid dreamer described a technique I've managed to adopt with time: anchoring yourself in a dream state by focusing all your attention on generating one specific object.

Here's the technique: pick an object that exists in the real world. (My friend chose a red rubber ball.) The object should be small enough to hold in the palm of your hand.

Once you select the object, hold it in your hand for several minutes. Let yourself become very familiar with the weight and shape of the object.

For the next several minutes, without picking the object up, re-create the sensation of holding the object in your hand as vividly as possible. Feel the weight. Feel the texture. Feel the contours of the object's shape. With your eyes closed, imagine the object is in your hand. See it. If it makes noise, hear it. If it has a scent, smell it. The goal is to convince yourself that the object is completely real. ("Once you practice this," my friend noted, "you may become so good at fooling yourself, that you're really surprised, when you open your eyes, to find that the object isn't really there!")

Having mastered this ability in the waking world, you can carry your talent with you to the dream state. When you feel control slipping away or when you feel yourself waking up, hold out your hand and generate your anchoring object. Just as you do when awake, see it, feel it, hear it, and smell it. Make it real.

This act of extreme focus often stabilizes the dream state and returns control to you. In addition, the anchor object you've chosen—the bright-red ball, the yellow lemon, the heavy metal flashlight—will often appear in your dream hand. This miraculous appearance will become yet another dream cue, reinforcing your conscious awareness that you're in a dream state.

Affirming

Just as they use affirmations to invite lucid dreams, some lucid dreamers tell me they use affirmations to enhance and maintain lucidity.

If you employ this technique, choose your affirmations in advance. Donna L. uses "I can take control at any time" and "I will wake when I'm ready." When a dream becomes threatening or when she encounters resistance to her will, she repeats "I can take control at any time" five times. When she feels herself waking up, she intones "I will wake when I'm ready."

Again and again, she (and others) report success with affirmations like these. Reinforce their availability by practicing them in the waking world. Then, when you need them in a dream, they'll be close at hand.

Chapter 6 in a Nutshell

Since every dream is a potential portal into the land of lucidity, paying careful attention to your dreams makes perfect sense.

Dream journals are a fun, convenient, and easy tool for enhancing dream awareness. In a dream journal, you can record your dreams in as much detail as suits you. You can use free-form methods (incorporating sketches and pictures) or, if you prefer, you can use a template to make recording your dreams as routine as possible. Choose your dream journal with care, as it needs to be accessible, portable, and durable. You'll also want to keep a good pen on hand and—because your dreams will often come to you in the darkness of your bedroom—a handy source of dependable, adequate light.

Reality checks—frequent pauses during which you ask, "Am I dreaming?"—can also greatly enhance your dream awareness. Choose one and stick with it, performing your reality check every time you walk through a doorway, spot a headline, or hear a clock chime. With time, you'll carry this practice into the dreamworld . . . and discover, to your delight, that you really *are* dreaming!

Having achieved a suitable degree of awareness, the next step toward lucidity involves maintaining dream consciousness and control. For most lucid dreamers, maintaining lucidity is a skill that grows over time; success is measured in degrees. Celebrate every step you take toward lucidity, and employ simple but effective techniques (spinning, anchoring, and affirming) to extend your ability to stay in—and stay in control of—your dreams.

What's Next?

Having boosted your awareness of dreams, now might be a good time to listen to the stories of other people who are experiencing lucidity on a regular basis. You'll find their stories—and tips on how to incorporate their wisdom into your own quest for lucidity—in chapter 7.

If you've begun having your own lucid dreams (or if you've been experiencing lucidity for some time), the gallery of applications for lucid dreaming in chapter 8 may offer you a number of engaging, exciting new experiments to try.

As part of focusing on your dreams—or as part of an effort to get more out of your lucid dreams—you may become curious about dream analysis. If so, chapter 9 provides everything you'll need to decode the symbols you encounter in dreams you control . . . and dreams you don't!

seven

In Their Own Words: Tips and Techniques from Lucid Dreamers

In this chapter, you'll discover:

- True stories as told by actual lucid dreamers
- Deeply personal insights into lucid dreaming
- Tips and techniques drawn from the experience of real-life lucid dreamers, designed to help you achieve lucidity more easily

It's one thing to read about a skill; it's another thing entirely to learn that skill directly from those who practice it. Want to learn glassblowing? Spend time with glassblowers. Want to learn to play guitar? Spend time with guitar players.

If you're serious about learning to lucid dream, you'll eventually want to find other lucid dreamers and learn from their experiences. In major cities, you can meet other lucid dreamers at dream awareness workshops and dream interpretation courses. Sessions like these are frequently hosted by colleges, holistic health centers, and alternative bookstores. If you live outside a major city, the Internet can be an invaluable tool for meeting and communicating with other lucid dreamers.

Until you make your own lucid dreaming acquaintances, you can learn a great deal from the lucid dreamers who volunteered to share their personal stories in this chapter. The following profiles are of actual people, although, in some cases, names and other details have been changed to protect the dreamers' privacy. They come from many different backgrounds, and all of them have different levels of comfort and achievement with lucid dreaming.

In addition to the profiles, you'll find specific tips and techniques, drawn from the experience of these lucid dreamers, that you can use as you continue your personal pursuit of lucidity.

Gina: The Relaxed Approach

Gina's Profile

Gina, forty-one, has only begun to have lucid dreams during the past two years. For her, the process is still new ... and more than a little frustrating. "Once I realize I'm having a lucid dream, I usually wake up! The lucid parts of my dreams last only a very short while. During a lucid dream, I feel rushed, because I'm so afraid I'll lose the experience!"

Currently, Gina manages to generate between three and five lucid dreams per year (though, she admits, "I could probably have more if I really put my mind to it"). She attributes her success to one very effective technique:

> If I wake up extremely early—around four a.m.—I try to take advantage of that by getting up and meditating for a half-hour or so before going back to sleep. Whenever I do this, I recall very vivid dreams and other unusual phenomena. It's also when I have most of my lucid dreams.

Gina perceives that her dreams are tricky, presenting familiar environments with such an extreme degree of reality that she fails to realize she's dreaming:

> The other night, I found myself in my mother's bedroom. Immediately, I suspected I was dreaming, and I started looking around the room, trying to find something that might be a dream cue. No matter how closely I studied the room, it appeared to be perfect in every detail.
>
> Then, I spotted something I couldn't believe I had overlooked. In the real world, you can walk right up to my mother's bedroom window. Here, there was a chest of drawers blocking it. Once I realized this, I noticed other problems, including a clock that always said half-past one.

Once she realizes she's dreaming, Gina takes advantage of the dreamworld's elastic reality and takes part in one of her favorite pastimes: flying.

> In my dreams, I'm always falling—in fact, I've begun to recognize extended, slow-motion falls as a dream cue. Most of the time, I can switch from falling to flying, turning a very frightening situation into a fabulous one. In one very early

lucid dream, I managed to fly through space at a phenomenal rate of speed. It was absolutely exhilarating!

Not long ago, I dreamed of being at a very busy party. As soon as I realized I was dreaming, everyone else in the room disappeared. Though I could assume enough control to explore the empty room, I couldn't find a way out, and willing one to appear just wasn't working.

Eventually, I just sat down on the sofa and amused myself by staring down at the outlandish carpet. Soon, the carpet disappeared, and I was whooshing through space. Remember that scene from *Star Wars*, when the Millennium Falcon jumps to hyperspace? It was just like that, with the stars becoming bright strips of light. It felt like being on one of those crazy, high-speed carnival rides.

When I woke up, I couldn't escape the sensation that I'd really experienced the flight. I was very disappointed to be back in my bedroom!

Gina was one of several lucid dreamers who reported that inaccuracies in the dreamworld—odd details that aren't quite right, like the chest of drawers blocking access to her mother's bedroom window—may turn out to have implications in the real world.

Shortly after I dreamed about Mother's bedroom, she decided to get rid of her old bedroom furniture. The next time I visited, she showed me her new chest of drawers. She had placed it right in front of her window! The new chest of drawers was blocking access to the window, just as it had in my dream.

Tips and Techniques from Gina's Story

- **Consider the value of a formal program.** Gina has chosen a more "laid back" approach to lucid dreaming, eschewing a formal program. She's experienced some success, but she's still not having lucid dreams as often as she'd like. Like Gina, you may discover that, with just a little focus, you can generate the occasional lucid dream. If increasing the frequency of those dreams is important to you, you may want to switch from a more casual approach to the more structured one described in this book.

- **Be persistent.** Lucidity takes time to achieve. Like Gina, you may feel your dreams, at first, are conspiring to deceive you with realistic environments and intriguing distractions. If you get into the habit of studying details and performing reality checks in the waking world, you'll eventually carry those habits over into the dreamworld. With time, patience, and practice, you'll begin to achieve lucidity more often.

- **When one technique fails, try another.** In the dreamworld, your experiences are limited only by your own creativity. When Gina found herself unable to locate or generate an exit to her sealed party room, she changed her tactics and settled in to enjoy the elaborate carpet pattern. Having done so, she effortlessly achieved her goal of escaping the room. If early attempts to control a dream fail, adopt her technique and turn your attention to something else entirely.

- **Have fun.** Lucid dreams present a remarkable opportunity to indulge in the broadest possible variety of thrills and fantasy. Fly. Race through space at the speed of light. Defy the laws of nature. Become a giant . . . or shrink yourself down to microscopic size. Even if you don't believe in it, give astral projection a try by visiting a distant place . . . or a distant planet! For lucid dreamers, the dreamworld is a playground. Whatever you fancy—have at it!

Johanna: Images and Insights

Johanna's Profile

Johanna Gargiulo-Sherman, an author and artist, created the popular Sacred Rose Tarot. Her lucid dreams began very early in life—so early, in fact, she cannot remember her first lucid dream. She does, however, recall one lucid dream from her childhood years that she found unusually comforting and powerful:

> I dreamed that I went into a world of bright white light. This world was accessed through a doorway located on the right side wall of our family's old Kelvinator refrigerator. On the other side of the doorway was a four-poster bed covered in white lace and starched cotton bedding. The room had an old-fashioned washstand with pitcher and basin. It felt very comfortable and welcoming to me.

Today, she enjoys one to three lucid dreams per week; about 95 percent of the dreams she remembers are lucid dreams. Like many lucid dreamers, Johanna has adopted a number of techniques over the years to increase the frequency of her lucid dreams. "Relaxation techniques in general have been helpful, and I've also used music or special recordings to 'program' myself to have a lucid dream. When I have a situation that is a challenge, I meditate on a question before going to sleep, and in my dreams, I'll receive an answer." In addition, Johanna claims that contacting entities she refers to as her guides can enhance her ability to achieve lucidity.

Like a number of lucid dreamers I spoke with, Johanna believes her lucid dreams, though under her control to an extent, can and do point her in important directions in the waking world. In one lucid dream, as she wandered through an antique store, she encountered a unique and striking individual:

> Behind the shop's counter was a man. He was overweight in a very soft and flabby way, with a round face and large round eyes. I was thinking to myself, "What a strange-looking man!" When I introduced myself, he spoke his name in return: "Seth."
>
> Because I found him interesting, I chose to chat with him a while. We had an interesting discourse, and, at one point, he paused and handed me a book with a curious title: *He Speaks*. When I asked what the title meant, he smiled and said that I would know soon enough.
>
> Weeks later, I received a gift from a friend: a copy of a book titled *Seth Speaks*. Inside was a drawing of Seth—the same man I met in my lucid dream!

Tips and Techniques from Johanna's Story

Johanna's experience suggests a number of techniques you could adopt and test as you pursue your own lucid dreams:

- **Create a comforting retreat.** During lucid dreams, your environment is completely malleable—yours to envision and create at will. Just as Johanna found comfort in the old-fashioned refuge she discovered inside the family refrigerator, you can summon up a secret hiding place tailor-made to your personal specifications. Do you recall a place where you felt particularly safe or empowered? Re-create it in your dream, and visit it as a way of relaxing yourself and refreshing your spirit.

- **Explore relaxation techniques.** Johanna adapted a number of relaxation techniques as lucid dreaming aids, and you can do the same. If a certain CD or MP3 helps you relax and fall asleep, consider how it might be used to ease you into a lucid dreaming state. You might also play a recording of your affirmations or lucid dream goals just before bedtime.

- **Incorporate your belief system.** Johanna mentioned contacting her guides as a means of encouraging lucid dreams. When threatened in a dream, she uses real-world magical practices—like casting a circle—to insure her safety. While your beliefs may differ from hers, you can always integrate expressions of your personal faith into your lucid dreaming practice. You could, for example, use prayer to encourage lucid dreams, or use your lucid dreams to visit holy

sites or view important moments in the history of
your faith.

- **Ask for guidance.** After meditating on questions,
  Johanna allows her dreams to provide answers. If
  you're facing a challenge, you can use lucid dreams
  to visit with a trusted friend, beloved relative, or even
  a custom-made wise advisor. You may discover that
  dream advisors often provide helpful, objective, and
  surprisingly insightful recommendations for dealing
  with real-world issues.

- **Watch for connections between the waking world
  and the dreamworld.** Johanna encountered "Seth"
  long before someone passed her a book composed
  of material allegedly dictated by an entity of the same
  name. When lucid dreaming, make a point to remember cryptic statements and odd references made by
  dream companions. These may not make sense at the
  time . . . but, if you record them, you may discover a
  correspondence between a dream character's com-
  ment and an event in the waking world.

Neal: Overcoming Fears

Neal's Profile

Neal regularly uses lucid dream techniques to seize control of nightmares and convert them into more pleasant
experiences. When confronted by terrifying monsters or
chased by dream creatures who seek to do him harm, he
escapes by "switching the scene."

During one nightmare, though, just as Neal started to switch to a safer situation, something unusual happened:

> Up to that point, the dream had been very convoluted, with lots of conflicting detail. I was running like a gazelle through an African delta, getting grassy and wet . . . but, at the same time, I knew I was in Denver, Colorado! I was being chased by a very large man made of driftwood, which sounds silly now, but which, during the dream, was very frightening. He was accompanied by a number of vicious wild dogs.
>
> As I ran, I passed many kids I've taught (most of whom are all grown up now) and several teachers and administrators I recognized from work. I was too busy running to speak to them, though . . . and, besides, each time I paused, I sank calf-deep in the water-logged earth.
>
> Then I noticed one of my dream cues: I was trapped in a sort of maze. Once I realized I was dreaming, I started to switch the scene—but before I could, I heard the voice of Walter Cronkite say, "Stay here! You *need* this dream!"
>
> Now, Walter's shown up before, so that's not so unusual. But he's never told me what to do, let alone ordered me to stay in a particular scene. To be honest, I was a little freaked out. I've never had the experience of being told not to change a dream before!

Wisely, Neal took Walter Cronkite's advice. He retained control . . . but, instead of switching scenes, he decided to just stop running.

> When I chose to listen to Walter, I realized I was standing in one of the most fertile places on earth: an African delta in Denver! I was struck with the potential of the place: the nourishing water, the lush growth, the bright sunshine,

and the fresh air. I got the impression I needed to take advantage of these perfect conditions before this perfect moment passed.

Meanwhile, the driftwood man caught up to me. As he approached, I could see he wasn't solid; in fact, I could see right through him. The closer he came, the smaller he appeared to be. By the time he walked up to me, I could see he was a child. I took his hand, and together, we watched all the wildlife in the delta.

Aware that this dream had special meaning, Neal recorded it in detail. Over the next two months, he felt its meaning became crystal clear:

I love teaching young children . . . it's my passion and delight. In evaluations, I routinely received the highest possible ratings and enjoyed seeing kids become excited about school and learning.

I left the public schools, though, after my principal told me that I would have to abandon the teaching style I'd crafted over the years and start teaching toward a particular test. (This, despite the fact that my kids already performed almost three times better on that test than other kids in our district!)

This dream came to me as I was deciding whether or not to go back into teaching. I've wanted to go back to the classroom for a long time, but I was afraid to do so. I was worried about working for a principal who can't think outside the "No Child Left Behind" box. I worried about coworkers resenting my previous decisions. And, to be honest, I was afraid that I wouldn't be a good teacher anymore . . . that, once I returned to the classroom, I'd fail.

In the end, I decided that, in running from the classroom, I was running from a "driftwood man" of my own making. When I stood my ground, my perspective changed, and I could suddenly see right through what had terrified me before.

The environment of the dream made sense, too. I'd considering "switching scenes" in real life by going somewhere else to teach. But the dream indicated to me that right here in Denver, I could be in the middle of the most fertile place on earth: a classroom! It's filled with potential: the water of dreams, the mud and growth of life, the sunshine of goals, and the fresh air of clear thoughts. Those are perfect conditions . . . but you have to take advantage of them before they dry up!

Neal is careful to note that these realizations didn't occur to him during the dream, but only after recording and reflecting on it:

I didn't realize all of this in the dream. Only later did I become conscious that kids need a pal like me to show them the wonders of the delta. It's my job to fill in that driftwood skeleton with books and math tricks and science experiments.

As a result of this dream, I learned it's not a bad thing to face my fears. I can overcome my own anxieties. My vision of education was reaffirmed.

Two weeks later, Neal returned to the classroom for the first time in years.

Tips and Techniques from Neal's Story

- **When danger lurks, change channels.** Lucid dreams can be powerful tools for overcoming nightmares and fears. Neal's ability to "change channels" frees him from the stress of threatening dream situations and gives him enormous confidence in the dreaming world. During your next nightmare, why not seize control? Transform your fears into friends and swap that spooky setting for a more soothing one.

- **Watch for dream cues.** Neal's dream self had no problem embracing the idea of an African delta in the middle of Colorado. Not even the appearance of children he'd taught years before—many of whom he now knows as adults—alerted him to the fact that something strange or unusual was going on. What finally caused him to "wake up" without waking up was the appearance of the maze—one of his recurring dream cues. By charting and becoming familiar with your own dream cues, you greatly increase the odds that you will achieve lucidity.

- **When dream guides speak, listen.** Over time, Walter Cronkite has emerged in Neal's dreams as a dream guide—a recurring figure who offers helpful advice. As you record your own dreams, you may notice that certain figures (celebrities, relatives, friends) appear again and again. People who take up persistent residence in your dreamworld can frequently become sources of wisdom and guidance. Even as you assume control of your dreams, pay close attention to what they have to say.

- **Face your fears.** Once you realize—on both a conscious and subconscious level—that you are generating your own dreams, you can begin to deal with

your dreams in new and exciting ways. As a lucid
dreamer, you know you can "change channels" at any
time. With this in mind, you may find that frightening dream entities aren't quite as threatening as they
were in times past. This kind of realization can give
you the courage to face your fears . . . and may lead
you to a new understanding of pesky anxieties and
lingering doubts.

- **Review and analyze your dreams.** Part of the joy of
  keeping a dream journal is rereading your entries
  at a later time. As you review your dreams, you may
  discover what, in retrospect, appear to be pointers to
  current events . . . or you may find that your present-
  day experience holds clues to the meaning of what, in
  the past, was a particularly puzzling dream.

Melinda and Ketutar: Cautious Control
Their Profiles

Melinda and Ketutar live very different lives. Melinda is an
American; Ketutar is Finnish. While Melinda is generally
agnostic, Ketutar describes herself as a witch. Both, though,
share an extremely cautious approach to the business of lucid dreaming.

Melinda began experimenting with lucid dreaming while
very young, primarily as a means of escaping a recurring
nightmare:

> I would be in a dark forest, and there would be four tall
> fir trees that would form a square with their trunks. When
> I got in the middle, big spiders would come down, make

webs between the trees, and trap me in there. Eventually, I started trying to think how I could get myself out of these nightmares. I remember opening my eyes really, really wide in the dream, trying to get my real eyes to open. Eventually, my eyes would open, but I would still be asleep. Light [from the real world] would filter in, and eventually wake me up for real.

With time, this "wake up technique" proved easier and easier to implement, and Melinda used it frequently when dreams became threatening or dull. As an adult, though, Melinda hesitates to exert control over her dreams:

I don't have trouble staying in the dream, if I want to. I mostly use [lucid dreams] as an opportunity to explore situations I'm facing in life and to gain subconscious knowledge that would be inaccessible when I'm awake.

I don't really try to control [my lucid dreams] now, despite the fact that I know I'm dreaming. I usually think there's some important message that's trying to come through, and I try to leave myself receptive to it. Especially during what I call anxiety dreams, which I have during very intense periods of my life, I think my dreams are trying to work out buried tension [and I wouldn't want to interfere with that process].

I do, though, like being able to wake myself up from unproductive dreams.

Ketutar had her first lucid dream when she was around twenty years old. Sixteen years later, she has lucid dreams very frequently, but doesn't experience—or desire—the degree of control reported by other lucid dreamers:

My lucid dreams are especially real . . . it's hard to know whether I'm awake or not. I remember reading a book about dreams and seeing that one can decide what one dreams. For me, it doesn't work very well. The dream follows its own course . . . the only thing I can affect is what I do. In other words, I can do exactly what I want, but the dream doesn't "do" what I want. I can only control myself, but I'm able to do anything, look how I want to look, wear what I want to wear, and go anywhere I please.

I always have the feeling that, if I try to lead my dreams, I'm interrupting the fine mechanics of the mind . . . something I fear will cause trouble later on. I read somewhere that dreams are the brain's way of sorting, arranging, and evaluating all the information and stimuli we encounter while awake.

Both of these women can easily achieve consciousness during the dream state. Even so, because they assign a great deal of significance to the content and potential healing properties of their dreams, they hesitate to assume outright control of dream events.

Tips and Techniques from Their Experiences

- **Control isn't everything.** For a variety of reasons, you may well decide that dream control isn't for you. You may, like Melinda and Ketutar, decide to be content with being able to know when you're dreaming. This knowledge alone can be very powerful, allowing you to pay special attention to your dreams (without influencing their content) and making it possible for you to "opt out" of nightmares at will.

- **The eyes have it.** During REM sleep, our muscles are paralyzed, most likely to prevent us from acting out

our dreams. The muscles controlling our eye movements, however, are not subject to this paralysis,
enabling us to experience the rapid eye movements
that characterize REM sleep. Like Melinda, you may
be able to put this "loophole" to work by leaving
a light on in your room. If you master her trick of
opening your real eyes by widening your dream eyes,
you may be able to use your nightlight as a reliable
cue for waking up.

- **Balance control with awareness.** Especially if you feel
  your dreams contain important symbolic, psychological, or spiritual messages, you may be interested
  in achieving a balance between "free dreaming" (allowing your dreams to control themselves) and lucid
  dreaming. You'll likely achieve this balance without
  trying, as very few people are able to achieve lucidity
  100 percent of the time! That said, if having a certain
  number of uncontrolled dreams is important to you,
  you might consider a routine that encourages free
  dreaming on certain nights of the week.

- **Do what's comfortable for you.** The greatest thing
  about the lucid dreaming state is its ability to tran-
  scend the rigid rules that govern our waking existence. I recommend you extend that sense of freedom
  to your pursuit of lucid dreams! Instead of thinking
  in terms of "right" or "wrong" ways to experience
  lucid dreams, think in terms of finding the approach
  that's right (or that works) for you. Instead of feeling
  you must perform certain tasks or achieve a specific

degree of control, embrace whatever opportunities lucidity brings your way. A relaxed approach will produce better results than a strained, stressful one.

Mark: Enthusiastic Experimentation

My Profile

As I mentioned in earlier chapters, I've always been fascinated by dreams and dreaming. My own experimentation with lucid dreaming is covered in detail in the Foreword to this book; elements of my personal lucid dreaming regimen are discussed in chapters 5 and 6. The tips and techniques offered here grew out of the experiences described in those passages.

Tips and Techniques from My Own Experience

- **Record every dream and dream fragment.** Not long after you start your dream journaling, you'll wake up with an elusive fragment of a dream in your head. "I was in a mall," you'll say. "But that's all I can really remember. Is that enough to write down?" The answer is an emphatic "Yes!" As you write that fragment down, you'll very naturally begin to remember the rest of the dream: "I was in a mall . . . shopping for Halloween costumes . . . when some sort of talking doll started offering me boxes of candy . . ." Show up at the page, and let the journal work its magic.

- **Don't edit dream journal entries.** When working with your dream journal, keep your goal in mind. You're not trying to win a Pulitzer; you're trying to enhance your dream recall. Concerns with spelling, punctuation, and proper grammar are inappropriate. If you make mistakes, don't erase, don't invest time and energy in elaborate scratch-outs, and don't, whatever you do, start over. Get the dream down. Nothing else matters.

- **Don't read your own journal entries for the first thirty days.** Looking back over a month's worth of entries is a real eye-opener! If you'll allow the entries to accumulate, you'll shock yourself in two unique ways. First, you'll be stunned at how many of your dreams, so vivid when you recorded them, have slipped away and been forgotten entirely. Second, you'll see patterns in your dreams—repeating themes, settings, people, and symbols—that you've never been aware of before.

- **Don't try all the techniques at once.** If your eagerness to have a lucid dream convinces you that "more is better," you can easily make the mistake of trying to adopt every single strategy in this book at once. Don't! If your routine is simple, you'll stick with it—so keep things simple. For the first thirty days, pick two or three lucid dreaming applications to focus on. You can always add others later on.

- **Be patient.** My innate orientation toward over-achievement almost kept me from having lucid dreams at all. Frankly? When I set out to start lucid dreaming, I expected to have my first one within a week—two weeks tops. In retrospect, I know that kind of thinking probably worked against me, delaying my success by generating inappropriate pressure. So take deep breaths . . . and take your time. Lucid dreams are worth the effort . . . and worth the wait.

Chapter 7 in a Nutshell

When learning about lucid dreaming, it makes sense to spend some time with lucid dreamers. You can usually make contact with other lucid dreamers through workshops, metaphysical bookstores, and holistic health centers. For those who lack access to resources like these, the Internet makes a perfectly good alternative meeting place.

Should you have trouble locating others who share your passion for dream control, this chapter summarizes the experiences of five very different lucid dreamers . . . and includes tips and advice gleaned from their quests to achieve lucidity.

What's Next?

Having learned about lucid dreams through other people's firsthand experience, you may want to explore the applications explored by those who enjoy lucid dreaming on a regular basis. These are outlined in detail in chapter 8, along with tips and techniques to help you achieve similar results.

Now would also be a great time to explore the analysis of dreams—both lucid and traditional. Chapter 9 provides a short, simple, but comprehensive overview of everything you need to know in order to conduct your own dream analysis.

eight

Applications of Lucid Dreaming

At some point, you will begin to have lucid dreams on a regular basis. Lucid activities that struck you as incredible the first few times—flying, changing shape, changing size, revising the world around you—may engage you less as they become more commonplace. Like many lucid dreamers, you may decide you want a challenge.

This chapter presents you with eleven applications for lucid dreaming—activities to try, goals to achieve, experiments to pursue. In addition to illustrations from actual dreams, you'll find specific tips and techniques you can use when trying these applications out in your own dreamworld.

Explore Alternate Realities

The Process

My own dreams—whether lucid or uncontrolled—often take place in what seem to be slightly off-kilter versions of my waking world. At times, I feel I'm eavesdropping on a parallel existence: a version of my own life, rooted in slightly different opportunities, coincidences, and choices.

Other people share this belief; a husband and wife in one of my dream workshops, for example, were convinced their dreams regularly "tune in" to alternate realities. Other lucid dreamers report experiences like these:

> I've been married to Rhonda for eight years. But in college, I dated Kerin for more than a year, and both of us believed we would end up together. One time (I still don't know what got into me), I picked up and went out with another woman behind Kerin's back. She found out about it and broke off our engagement.
>
> More than once, I've used lucid dreams to get back to my college days and spend time with Kerin, who I still have a thing for. I also like to use lucid dreams to build a full-scale replica of my life, but with Kerin as my wife, just to see what could have been.
>
> —*Kerin, 36*

* * * * *

More than anything else, I wanted to become an artist and even applied to an art school. But Mother got sick, and I stayed home, and now all that's water under the bridge. In my dreams, though, I go back, make mother healthy, and get to see what life would have been like if I had been able to keep that commitment to myself.

Looking back at what I've written, it sounds pretty morbid or depressing. It's not. In fact, seeing how happy I can be in those dreams where I make myself into an artist has gotten me to thinking that maybe it's not too late to give art school a try.

—*Gwen, 31*

* * * * *

Most of my dreams take place at home or at the office. When I realize I'm dreaming, it's fun to rearrange things. I'm usually the boss, and I give myself that office on the corner of the fifth floor, where I can see the deli and the theater. I've done a lot of work in that office. As weird as it sounds, both in my dreams and at work, I sometimes feel that I really do belong in that space, or that I've been there in some other life, or that I'm going to be there before it's all over.

—*Beth, 47*

Tips and Techniques

Meditation. As you slip into sleep, let your mind drift back to one of those life-changing moments. In your mind's eye, allow yourself to make a different decision: go (or don't go!) on that particular date, accept (or turn down!) that job, or spend (or don't spend!) that last summer at home before going off to college.

In your mind's eye, allow yourself to see, in as much detail as possible, the impact of your new choice. What people do you meet? What people would you never meet? What places would you go? What things would you do? How would your life differ?

Allow these details to serve as a road map during your next lucid dream. Once you assume control, change the setting and characters, make the change you want to make, and see what happens. Remember, too, that you can "advance the clock" at any point in time and see where your new choices take you.

Through the looking glass. Adapting the reality check technique, throughout your day pause occasionally to see if you've shifted from one universe to the other. Look for small details that might indicate that you've made such a shift: words spelled differently, photographs with edited details, or people who seem familiar, even though you've never met them.

In your next lucid dream, look for similar dream cues— signs that the world around you, despite its similarity to the waking world, differs in some significant way from conscious reality. If you prefer, take control: summon a doorway designed to allow you to travel "through the looking glass" and into a parallel world. While maintaining consciousness, see what forms and shapes this alternative reality will assume.

Travel Beyond Your Body

The Process

Keith Harray and Pamela Weintraub's *Lucid Dreams in Thirty Days* has often been criticized for linking lucid dreaming to the practice of astral travel and the pursuit of OBE's, or "out of body experiences."

While I have no personal experience with astral travel or OBEs, many of the people who attend my dream workshops or who shared their lucid experiences with me claim to have done so. Many of these link their practice to the achievement of lucidity.

* * * * *

In my dreams, my feet never quite touch the floor for some reason. I use that as one of my dream cues. So, this time, once I was having a dream, I just stopped everything I was doing and stood absolutely still. As a dream test, I decided I would try to rise up and fly through the ceiling.

I was completely unprepared for what happened next. I did rise up, but I had the distinct impression that I was "pulling loose." My spirit came out of my dream body. It felt like I was something warm and smooth, like a length of silk cloth being pulled up out of a plastic husk. Before I knew what to do, I was drifting just above my own body, looking down at myself.

At first, I panicked and started to lose the dream. I was very afraid that, if I woke up while out of my body, I might not find my way back into it. So I started spinning around in circles, trying to stay there. It worked. I stayed there, but I still wasn't in my body.

After getting over the fright, though, I discovered I could still move around and even leave the room. I got the impression that my body would wait for me, that it was sleeping when I was out, and that it would be there when I got back. So I glided around the neighborhood, all of which seemed frozen. I wondered whether being outside my body made time stand still somehow.

Back in my room, I slipped back into my body by centering myself over it and drifting slowly down. Even in the dream, coming back to a physical form made me feel heavy and clumsy—half paralyzed. I made sure my arms and hands and legs worked before waking myself up.

—*Dianne, 47*

* * * * *

As a kid, I really believed it when people said we'd have lunar colonies by 1997, and as an adult, I've been disappointed that we haven't done more with space travel. When I meditate, I often see stars. In one of my lucid dreams, I wanted to see the same cool, black expanse, so I said, "I'll just go into space."

Instead of just seeing stars, I was suddenly moving through them at this incredible rate of speed. At first, I didn't like it, because I felt like I was falling. Eventually, though, I found I could change direction and speed whenever I wanted to.

Since then, I've gone "star sailing" dozens of times—it's probably my favorite thing to do. Being able to leave my physical body and project myself into distant places is one of the best things about having dreams I control.

—*Barry, 41*

Tips and Techniques

Waking meditation. As part of a waking meditative practice, try projecting yourself into a distant space. Use waking meditation to practice feeling comfortable outside the confines of your physical body and to grow accustomed to the sensation of moving around without the constraints of a physical form.

If you do not meditate regularly, you can substitute focused daydreaming or intense imagination for meditation and achieve the same results. For several days in a row, as vividly as possible, picture yourself outside your body and in a distant space. Move around in this space using nothing more than your own strength of will. Free yourself from the idea that arms and legs are necessary to shift your position and point of view.

The next time you achieve lucidity, recall the sensations associated with your waking forays into out-of-body travel. In your dream, re-create those conditions. You may find that here, in the dreamworld, the sensations are far more intense than they ever are during meditative or imaginative sessions, so be prepared to be a little overwhelmed at first.

Personal projection. In your next lucid dream, why not take those first small steps toward astral projection? Center yourself in a space where you feel safe and comfortable. Then, while being careful to preserve the reality of the dreamworld, start "rotating" your astral body. (One woman reported that she imagines that her soul looks like a tornado or a vortex, with her consciousness centered in the "eye.")

Once you feel confident and focused, try to shift your awareness beyond the confines of your dream body. Some people find it useful to generate graphic imagery—picturing, for example, their heads opening like hinged containers or their chests opening like a cabinet.

As you slip away, turn back and inspect your own body. How does it look? How does it feel? What signs of your own absence can you detect? Pay attention, too, to how your nonphysical form feels. Summon a mirror to your dream room. What do you look like (if anything) while outside yourself? The answer may surprise you ... and yield insights that will be useful in the waking world, to boot.

Dream destinations. Using postcards, pictures from magazines, or images from the Internet, construct a dream destination for yourself. Combine elements of several of your favorite places. What if New York were on the beaches of the Florida coast? What if your neighborhood was a suburb of Paris? What if your current home could be surrounded by gardens, mountains, rain forests, and lush waterfalls? What if your view of the sky could include multiple moons, the distant lights of a space platform, or the golden clouds of Nirvana?

Assemble your image (or, if you prefer, write about it, paint it, or model it in some way). Keep it beside your bed as a dream token. Before going to sleep, spend at least ten or fifteen minutes gently focusing your attention on your destination. What will it feel like to be there? What will you do? What aspect of your destination are you most eager to explore? What other people will meet you there?

In your next lucid dream, assume control and, as vividly as possible, re-create your dream destination in the dreamworld. You may discover, as several lucid dreamers have, that your efforts to see this place as clearly as possible in the waking world help you re-create it in remarkable detail in your dreams.

Communicate with the Dead

The Process

Our dreams regularly pierce the veil that separates this world from the world inhabited by ancestors and loved ones who have passed away. My own father, dead now for fifteen years, regularly appears in both my uncontrolled and lucid dreams. Friends report being approached by deceased parents, brothers and sisters, and even ancestors they never knew.

In some cultures, these visitations are taken very seriously, and the dead who appear in dreams are assumed to be the actual spirits of those who have left this world for another. Some believe the dreamworld does allow departed loved ones to communicate directly with us; others discount the experience and consider it little more than wish-fulfillment.

Reality? Fantasy? Ultimately, it may not matter. After I meet my father in my dreams, I feel comforted and closer to him. He gives me good advice. I wake up feeling happier and more "at home." For me, those benefits greatly override any questions about the objective reality of the experience.

* * * * *

In the dream, I'm walking our dog in the grassy area behind our apartment. It's the last walk of the day, the one we take just before bed, with the city very dark and very still. There's a moon high in the sky overhead, and I'm looking up at the stars.

Suddenly, I realize that, despite the late hour, the trees and buildings around me are lit exactly as they are in the daytime, despite the black sky. Right away, I know I'm dreaming. For the last several weeks, I've been hoping to dream about my father, so I think of him and picture him walking toward me.

At that moment exactly, he comes around the corner of the condo, smiling, whistling, and jangling his keys and coins in his pocket (a habit of his). He is about the age he was when he died, or perhaps a little younger. He hugs me. Even though I've arranged these meetings in many other lucid dreams, I'm amazed at the complete reality of this experience. His strength, his warmth, his scent—everything about him is totally real.

With time, we're no longer in the backyard; we're sitting at a café on a street in what I think is Paris. Still, I remain focused on maintaining contact with him, and we manage to have a long conversation about the decisions I'm facing in my life.

—*Mark, 41*

* * * * *

Since I came out, my sister and I have always wondered what our mother would have thought about my being a lesbian. My sister is a lucid dreamer—always has been. The next time she had a lucid dream, she deliberately went looking for my mother, found her in the florist shop where she worked, and asked her about it.

My sister said Mother shrugged off the news entirely. "Doesn't matter to me," Mother said. "That sort of thing isn't important here." My sister tried again and again to get more details, but Mother wouldn't hear of it. "It's just not important," she kept saying. "Let's talk about something else."

While my sister was disappointed, I thought this sounded exactly like what my mother, with the perspective of having passed over, would say and do. I'm convinced she made some sort of real contact, and no one can tell me any different.

—*Pat, 53*

Tips and Techniques

Ancestral altars. Adapt the dream token practice to your goal by decorating a bedside table with photographs of the deceased person you wish to contact. If you have personal objects that belong to him or her or gifts this person gave you, place these on the table as well. A candle, incense, or soft light adds atmosphere. (If you use a candle, be sure to extinguish it before you go to sleep.)

Before going to sleep, invite this person into your dreams. You might attempt to communicate silently with him or her, sending out a sort of prayer. You might also envision the two of you meeting and talking. As always, the goal is to see this moment as clearly and vividly as possible. As you fall asleep, gently return your attention to this image. Don't use force—just tell yourself how nice it would be to see this person again.

Watch for dream cues. As soon as you see one or as soon as you achieve lucidity, bring your friend or family member to mind. Will this person to appear, or call out and invite him or her to come out and see you. Once you are reunited, you may find it helpful to focus your consciousness on maintaining contact . . . even if doing so allows the setting of your dream to drift.

Writing letters. One young man shared this technique with me: before he attempts to meet his grandmother in a lucid dream, he writes her a letter. In the letter, he expresses the questions he wants help with or describes the events of his life. Later, he places the letter in an envelope. Sometimes, he actually mails the blank envelope. Other times, he places the envelope under his pillow or beside her photo.

"The letter tends to turn up in dreams," he says. "Once I realize I'm dreaming, I look for my grandmother, hand her the envelope, and she reads it. Sometimes she already knows what's in it. For me, writing the letter either brings her into my dream or helps me remember to call for her about nine times out of ten."

Consult Dream Guides

For those who believe in them, dream guides can be powerful allies, advocates, and advisors. A dream guide is a person, spirit, or animal that, in the dreamworld, appears to possess an unusual amount of insight and wisdom. For many lucid dreamers, the primary advantage of mastering lucid dreams is the ability to summon and consult dream guides at will.

I think of my own father as a dream guide and regularly seek his counsel. Other lucid dreamers fabricate dream guides out of whole cloth, preferring to design one to their own specifications. At least two other lucid dreamers tell me they simply ask for a dream guide ... and one always appears.

* * * * *

When I have a lucid dream, there's a place I like to go that's out in the Muir Woods. Once, when I was walking through the woods and admiring the giant redwood trees, a wolf came bounding out of the underbrush and blocked my path. At first, this spooked me, and I started to change him into something else ... but something in his expression made me pause.

I've met animals in dreams before, but this particular wolf comes across as conscious, even ancient. He comes when he wants to, not necessarily when I summon him. (I can make other wolves, but not this particular wolf.) Whenever he appears, he whines and paces until I'll follow him, and then he always takes me to see something important: a picture or a place. Almost invariably, I'll see that picture or place the next day.

—*Kel, 48*

* * * * *

I've started visiting this place I stumbled on while having a desert dream: a tented palace with thick rugs and big pillows inside. There are three men in there, in jeweled robes and big turbans. It sounds crazy, but I've come to think of them as personal advisors. I mean, it's like they're waiting there for me to show up.

Once I arrive, they always welcome me with a pipe and invite me to talk. I've tried to take them with me to other places, but they've told me not to do so, so I just describe my situation, and they give me tips on how to handle things at work or things at home. It's weird. Their advice is usually pretty good advice.

—*Stephen, 22*

Tips and Techniques

Define your guide. You can use collage, paint, a sketch, or other visual art to define your dream guide, creating a dream token to keep beside your bed. Referring to the token and meditating on it as you fall asleep can help you remember to create and consult your dream guide once you enter a lucid dream.

Alternatively, you might consider this simple exercise. On a sheet of paper, create a two-column table. In one column, write down notes describing your dream guide's personal appearance. What does he or she (or it!) look like? What clothing does he or she wear? What shape does he or she take? What environment does he or she prefer?

In the second column, define your dream guide's qualities: personality, demeanor, sense of humor, amount of patience. How should your dream guide act? What are his or her motivations, hopes, fears, and prejudices?

Having defined your dream guide, spend at least fifteen minutes a day imagining interactions with him or her. If you're facing an issue, ask, "What would my dream guide recommend?" Make a habit out of picturing and consulting your guide; if you do, you'll have an easier time summoning your guide in your next lucid dream.

Prefer to accept whatever guide the universe sends you? Make your desire known, and invite a guide into your lucid dreams, remaining open to whatever experience comes your way.

Guide checks. Remember how reality checks can help you remember to evaluate the world around you by prompting you to look for dream cues? Guide checks can achieve much the same thing, sensitizing you to watch for the appearance of a dream guide.

During your day, especially when people-watching, pause to ask, "Could that person (or animal) be my dream guide?" Seriously consider the question. What kind of advice would such a guide offer? What action would this person or animal take if, indeed, he or she were making an appearance in a dream as your guide?

Habit's the key. After you continue this practice for some time, you'll eventually ask the dream guide questions while dreaming. Once you realize you're asleep, you can approach the dream guide you've just spotted ... or summon one you've designed to meet your personal needs.

Experiment with Dream Communication

The Process

If you know of other friends or family members who are pursuing lucid dreams, you may wish to experiment with using lucid dreams as a form of communication.

The concept is simple. You and a companion, both of whom should be lucid dreamers, each compose a short, three- or four-word message. The best messages will be unusual and memorable; likely phrases ("I love you" or "It's me") should be avoided. In the waking world, you should keep these messages a secret from each other.

Once you achieve lucidity, deliberately seek out or summon your companion. In the dream, share your messages. As soon as the messages are exchanged, wake yourself up and record the message immediately.

* * * * *

My boyfriend and I have tried several times to exchange messages in the dreamworld. It's kind of neat thinking about the fact that, while we're lying together in bed, we're also reaching out to each other in our dreams.

I have lucid dreams a lot more often than he does, so that makes things harder. I've managed to find him in a lucid dream twice. Both times, I gave him the message, and he seemed to understand what I was doing, but when we woke up, he didn't remember having a dream, lucid or not.

I'd like to see what would happen if we both had a lucid dream on the same night.

—*Leesa, 21*

* * * * *

I have a personal goal of achieving dream communication with my cousin, who lives in San Francisco. Whenever I have a lucid dream, I imagine visiting her at home. In the dream, I always try to tell her something that she might remember, and then I call her the next day to see if she does.

Twice, she's had a dream about me on nights I had a lucid dream about her. She even dreamed I gave her a message and that she received it and was happy about it, but when she woke up, she couldn't remember what it was. Even she said, though, that she felt more like she dreamed about it because we've talked about it so much . . . not because I was really meeting her in the dream.

We'll keep trying. I've had dreams that told me she was upset, and I've had dreams that let me know she needed me. It's not much of a stretch to think we'll manage to talk to each other if we stick with it.

—*Paula, 47*

Tips and Techniques

Visualization. If you decide to work with the message exchange technique, spend several minutes a day visualizing the exchange in detail. While keeping the content of your message confidential, both of you should imagine making contact. Rather than imagine the actual content of the message passed along by your companion (you don't want to program yourself to see a certain message), allow yourself to feel the excitement and pride associated with a successful exchange.

Dream tokens. Write down your secret message, seal it in an envelope, and place it near your bed or under your pillow. As you go to sleep each night, hold the envelope and repeat the message to yourself several times. Remind yourself that the message is close by, and imagine yourself retrieving it and passing it along to your companion.

Scheduling. In addition to composing a message to share, you and a companion might also define a particular place and time in which to meet in the dreamworld. Pick a place both of you can easily visualize. Before going to bed each night, touch base with your dream companion, review your meeting plans, and meditate on the meeting as you fall asleep. When you achieve lucidity, summon your meeting place and create the conditions (time, weather, etc.) that the two of you agreed to in the waking world.

Dream Analysis

The Process

For traditional dreamers, dream analysis has been a passive exercise. The dreamer, at the mercy of the dream, encounters a series of symbols. These symbols are then interpreted after the fact, with dreamers or therapists assigning meaning according to any of several psychological, mythological, or personal systems.

Lucid dreaming offers an opportunity to participate more actively in the process of dream analysis. Instead of guessing at meanings after the dream concludes, lucid dreamers can assume control and interview the people, entities, and objects they confront in their dreams, asking, "What do you mean? What message do you have for me?" Puzzling dreams can be re-created and revisited in the lucid state, allowing dreamers to pursue additional information at their leisure.

* * * * *

I was having a typical nightmare, complete with rising water and the sound of something huge and invisible coming toward me out of the darkness. I have this dream so often, it's become a dream cue. Some of the time, I think, "I'm having that dream again," but I don't become lucid ... I just hunker down and get ready for whatever's coming. This time, though, I realized I was dreaming, and I decided to try something different.

When the thuds and crashes came closer, I shouted, "What are you? Come out and let me see you!" Everything went quiet, even the water. When I shouted my questions again, I heard a very distant voice, almost an echo, say, "Tomorrow."

I think of the rising water dream as one of my stress dreams, but I never really noticed how often having it coincides with the end of the sales quarter. It's crazy for me to be so stressed about that, because I always hit my targets, but hearing everyone else talk about not making their quotas always freaks me out. The last day of the quarter actually was the very next day.

Since I thought to ask that question, I haven't had that particular dream again.

—Keith, 24

* * * * *

Most lucid dreaming books emphasize the more common lucid dream practices: flying and sex. When I began talking with people about their lucid dreams, I was surprised at the wide variety of applications people reported. I started wondering, "What does it mean if someone tends to use a lucid dream to visit a dead relative? What might it mean if someone, given the chance to do anything at all, without limits or repercussions, chooses to spend most of his or her time in outer space?"

Looking back over my own lucid dream records, I found myself turning again and again to two pastimes: meeting friends I've lost touch with and traveling to foreign destinations. In the context of my waking life, I think my lucid dreams point to two important issues: a desire to expand my circle of friends and a very real feeling of dissatisfaction with where I'm living now. Both of those are things I can do something about, but I wouldn't have considered either of them to be important if I hadn't reviewed my own lucid dreaming records.

—Mark, 41

Tips and Techniques

Reality checks. When you encounter something unusual or out of the ordinary in the waking world, cultivate the habit of asking, "What could this mean?" In addition to sensitizing you to synchronicities (meaningful coincidences) in your waking life, this practice will make you more likely to ask the same question of objects and events in your lucid dreams.

Remember: in lucid dreams, real-world rules don't apply. You can ask a question of—and expect an answer from—inanimate objects, animals, and even environments. With this in mind, you can go beyond merely wondering, "What does this mean?" and teach yourself to expect an answer.

Dream journaling. Many people worry that lucid dreaming may interfere with the reception of important messages from the subconscious. Even lucid dreams, though, can provide valuable insights into your personality, psychology, and character.

When you have a lucid dream, what do you do? Where do you go? Whom do you choose to see? The answers to questions like these can be analyzed just as easily as the contents of a more traditional dream ... and can prove equally revealing.

After keeping a dream journal for several months, go back and reread only those entries associated with lucid dreams. What patterns do you detect? What insights can you glean?

Heal Yourself

The Process

Lucid dreams, with their remarkably vivid images and ability to simulate any reality, can be used as powerful tools for healing both the body and soul.

* * * * *

I've been struggling for years with high blood pressure. In my lucid dreams, I've created a private space: very calming, very reassuring, very safe. When I have a lucid dream, I invariably go there, sit in front of the window facing the sea, and meditate.

I meditate when I'm awake, too, but when I meditate during a dream, I tend to rise slowly off the pillows and float gently in the air. The feeling is incredible—very freeing, very relaxing. For those minutes, I'm outside the pull of gravity and feel completely at peace.

When I wake up from this dream, I feel like I've spent a week at a spa. My blood pressure's better than ever.

—*Philesha, 34*

* * * * *

I've used guided visualization as a way of controlling pain for several years now. In lucid dreams, I can take that a step further. Instead of seeing what I want to heal, I can actually go there. I can be inside my joints, and I can will away the inflammation. For me, that works better than copper bracelets or even Tylenol.

—*Janice, 57*

* * * * *

It's been more than twenty years and we lost touch afterward. My mind keeps going back, though, to my best
friend Amiee and the fight we had during our sophomore
semester. We were like sisters before that, and we never
spoke after.

Over the years, I've always wanted to make things right
and admit my part in what went wrong. I wonder about
Aimee, but I've been unable to find her.

In one lucid dream, I went back in time and, instead
of fanning the flames like I did then, I just admitted to
her what I had done wrong. In the dream, she was very
understanding. When I woke up, I felt better than I'd felt
about the situation in years, and I also felt like I'd had a
visit from Aimee.

I know now, when I really do see her, I'll be ready to
say what should have been said a long time ago.

—*Tracey, 39*

Tips and Techniques

Affirmations. As you continue your work with lucid
dreams, incorporate health-related affirmations into your
daily routine. Saying "I look forward to seeing and reliev-
ing the source of my pain" or "I can focus my energy and
heal myself while dreaming" prepares you to pursue these
goals when you achieve lucidity.

Visualizations. The same visualization and meditation techniques that supplement healing in the waking world can be
used to encourage health-focused lucid dreams. Devote fifteen to twenty minutes a day to visualizing, as vividly as possible, the health-related lucid dream you desire.

Picture yourself having a dream, encountering a dream
cue, becoming conscious, and taking control. Imagine that,

once you achieve lucidity, you visit the time, place, or area of your body that has become unproductive or unhealthy. Take appropriate action, and end your meditation with an exploration of how satisfied you'll be when you achieve this goal in a lucid dream.

Dream tokens. Dream tokens can be especially effective when the healing you desire is associated with a relationship. Make a collage, find a photograph, or retrieve a personal item associated with the person with whom you desire a reconciliation or confrontation. Frame the collage or photo or keep the object associated with that person on a bedside table.

Each night, just before going to sleep, hold the object in your hands and spend five minutes picturing the person connected with it. When you meet him or her, what will you say? How will you act? What questions will you have? What answers will you seek?

As you drift off to sleep, keep your attention gently focused on these issues.

Nightmare Management

The Process

Nightmares are polar opposites of lucid dreams: terrifying, threatening, or painful dreams that imprison the dreamer in a dark reality of his or her own creation. A nightmare takes the enormous potential of the dreamworld—the idea that anything can happen—and turns it against us. The monsters we encounter, the losses we suffer, and the pain we endure during a nightmare is all too real. Even after we wake up, our hearts pounding, recovery may take hours . . . or even days.

Lucid dreams provide us with new tools for facing our fears. By assuming control of our nightmares, we can alter dream environments, delete threatening elements, and dispel horrific characters. We can summon protectors . . . or transform ourselves in ways that allow us to meet and overcome the challenges a nightmare sends our way.

* * * * *

All through childhood, I was plagued by nightmares: awful dreams of being chased, kidnapped, held down, smothered. Early on, I learned the trick of rubbing my closed eyelids to "change the channel."

When my children were little, I taught them to do the same. My son took the process a step further. He would go back to sleep and summon a herd of stuffed animals to come and chase his monsters away.

—*Cathy, 35*

* * * * *

While living alone in a new city, I constantly dreamed that intruders were breaking into my house. I would wake up completely hysterical, convinced that a dark figure had just walked into the room and was looming over my bed. Neighbors said they could hear me screaming.

I remembered having a few lucid dreams during college, and a chat buddy suggested I try taking control of the dream instead of being victimized by it. The first two times, this didn't work. I was paralyzed in the bed, eyes open, watching the man come closer.

I don't know why—maybe I was getting used to the idea of having the dream—but the next time I had it, I said to myself, "Okay, this is just a dream." And just like that, something inside me relaxed. It literally felt as though something twisted up inside got released. In the dream, the lights came on. I realized how much I missed my roommate from back home, and I changed the intruder into him.

I never had the nightmare again.

—Chris, 22

Tips and Techniques

Visualization. Particularly helpful with recurring nightmares, a visualization (performed while you're awake) allows you to practice assuming control of a bad dream from the safety of the waking world.

With eyes closed and body relaxed, summon up your nightmare. Relive it in as much detail as possible, paying special attention to the emotions you feel as the dream unwinds. At what point does the nightmare become especially threatening or painful? When does your pulse quicken? When does your breathing become more rapid? When do you feel unsafe or afraid?

With that moment identified, wipe your mental slate clean and replay the dream. This time, however, at the moment of highest tension, imagine taking control of the dream and defeating any threatening elements. Trounce the monster. Change the attacker into a friendly puppy. Wipe the collapsing bridge away and replace it with a tranquil forest scene.

Many dreamers find pairing their assumption of control with a particular physical signal—giving a "thumbs up" or pointing their index finger—particularly effective. When they take charge of the imagined nightmare, they perform the gesture with their real-world hand.

Perform this waking visualization as often as time allows. Eventually, when you encounter the nightmare in the dreamworld, you will reflexively perform the physical signal . . . and assume control of the dream.

Dream tokens. Instead of creating a dream token representing your *desire* to experience a lucid dream, try constructing a dream token that serves as a symbol of your *ability* to control your dreams. Place the dream token by your bedside as a visual reminder of your achievement of lucidity.

During your waking hours, whenever you feel slightly threatened or stressed, make a habit of bringing your dream token to mind. Picture yourself holding it; imagine using it to assume control of the situation and warding off whatever bothers you.

As you drift off to sleep, gently draw your attention to a mental picture of your dream token. Carry the image with you into the dreamworld, and deploy it against any force that threatens you.

Rituals. Coming up with a response to a nightmare situation while still in the nightmare can prove challenging. When being pursued or threatened, you might not be at your most creative.

Rituals to the rescue! While awake, establish one universal response that you will call on again and again when faced with nightmare elements. You might decide, for example, that you will always change monsters into cute bunnies. You might decide that, when threatened, you will always fly away. You might elect to picture a single, simple "safe space" that you can retreat to in an instant.

Practice this ritual with visualizations; in the waking world, imagine yourself using the ritual to deal with awkward or threatening situations. Eventually, you will recall the ritual in a nightmare, where it will work to your advantage.

Recover Past Lives

The Process

Do you believe in reincarnation? Some insist that using lucid dreaming to regress beyond the moment of birth provides them with glimpses of previous lives. Others assert these "past life" dreams provide more insight into personal psychology than personal history. Whatever the case, past life recovery can provide you with powerful, highly emotional experiences.

* * * * *

I'm just outside what must be a medieval village. From the hill where I'm standing, I can see a rough circle of cramped houses with thatched roofs, all gathered around a muddy well. Several have chimneys, and I can see thin gray smoke rising from each one.

The morning is gray, and the clouds are low. I'm cold. I look down, see that I'm wearing a coat of tanned animal hide, and instantly realize that I'm dreaming. This is a very strange sensation for me, because, even though I know I'm dreaming, I also feel very much at home. There's a rightness about being on top of this hill, this early, on a cold, wet morning.

I've been here before—several times before. This is a city and a hillside I come to again and again in my dreams. It's not always this moment. The weather and times of year change, and the village is sometimes smaller, or sometimes larger, but always recognizable. I know that other people here call me "Tanner." I also know that, on this day, I'm supposed to be meeting several other men on the other side of this hill.

I top the hill, and I can see the other men waiting for me, stamping their feet and shifting their weight from leg to leg in an effort to keep warm. Like me, they're bearded and stout, with the exception of one stringy, unpleasant man I've met a few times before. The second I see him, I'm filled with anger, as though I've carried a grudge against him all my life.

Because I'm aware I'm dreaming, I briefly consider flying down to them, which is something I like to do. It occurs to me, though, that doing so would be inappropriate somehow—that these people would be terrified or scared or that flying might not even work. So I trudge down the hill. As I come nearer, I see each man is holding what looks like a loop of rope on the end of a long stick. I've never seen this kind of thing in the real world, but right away, I know the tool is some kind of rabbit snare.

Sure enough, as soon as I get to them, the men get down to business: trudging through the marshy grass, whacking the ground with sticks, and startling rabbits. We do this with the sort of speed and ease that comes from having hunted rabbits this way all of our lives. Even after I wake up, I can feel the weight and the urgency of the rabbit at the end of my snare, and I'm still concerned that he'll escape and that I won't have any meat today.

—Glen, 38

* * * * *

The dream I'm having is awful. It's a bank dream. I have them all the time. I'm at my teller window. People are cashing checks. I look down at the checks and realize I've cashed the same one over and over. I realize I'm dreaming, and I push everything and everyone away. I call it "blank slating." Just me, just the dark.

I know already where I'm going, so I picture the prairie grass and the big sky. As soon as I do, I realize I'm in a cave. I can see light up ahead. At the entrance, I can see the prairie, exactly as I pictured it. The wagons are up ahead. I can smell cookfires and horses.

I go here all the time. I don't think I'm me. It's like I'm inside someone else, seeing through her eyes. There's a log house I go to every time, with hard-packed dirt floors. On cold nights, the wind moans around it and gets through cracks in the mud between the logs. I know it's my responsibility to keep the house going and that people here don't like me wandering off to that cave all the time. How can I know all these details, if I've never been here before?

—*Anna Beth, 24*

Tips and Techniques

Pre-sleep meditation. As you drift off to sleep, open yourself to seeing and visiting a past life. One young woman in one of my dream workshops said, "This is a little bit like prayer. I just tell the universe that I'm ready, that I want to see where I've been before and what I did there. I focus on this as I fall asleep. When I do this for several nights in a row, I wind up dreaming about a prior life, and I can use my lucidity to explore it more fully, find people to talk to, and try to uncover details I could confirm with research."

False positives. During the day, as you walk through a familiar place or perform some mindless task, pretend that you are actually a future self, revisiting a past life (your current life) while dreaming in the future. See the world around you with your future self's eyes: savor flavors, absorb sights and sounds, and recall as much detail as possible. Give your future self a guided tour of your current (and his or her past) life. Make this a habit, and you'll find yourself engaging in the ritual, even in your dreams. With it, you can advance your pursuit of lucidity and enhance your efforts to recover past lives, as well.

Regression. Once you achieve lucidity in the dream state, try making yourself progressively younger. Find a mirror or hold out your hand. Watch your skin soften and thicken, and watch your features shift as you reach your twenties, your teens, your childhood. Keep going. Become an infant. Shrink even smaller, becoming an embryo, a blastula, and a single cell. Once in the dark, prepare yourself to "jump in" on the last moments of a previous life, willing it to happen. (Use this technique with care; past lives, I'm told, don't always end gently. Remember at all times that you're in control and that you can change or escape the situation without harm.)

Practice Anything

The Process

While in the corporate world, I was responsible for designing and managing complex training sessions. As a way of anticipating potential pitfalls before an event took place, I would hold virtual rehearsals—what I called "practice sessions"—in my head. By the time the session actually took place, I would have lived through it dozens of times.

I still draw on the technique today, using visualizations to anticipate questions, objections, or issues that may arise in workshops or presentations. Lucid dreaming, of course, helps me take practice sessions to the next level. Imagining a rehearsal is one thing; living through it in the dreamworld's virtual reality is quite another.

In one of my lucid practice sessions, a dream participant seized the floor for a question and wouldn't let go. I've lived through this in the real world, and it's a difficult situation to handle. You want to show respect for someone's viewpoint and opinion; at the same time, you want to prevent any one participant from monopolizing the workshop.

In this dream, the participant was expressing her opinion on how a particular Tarot card should be read. After giving her several minutes to make her point, I gently prompted her by saying, "That's a fascinating take on the subject. Let's hear what some others have to say."

The dream participant dismissed me with a wave of her hand. "I'm making a point," she said, and she kept right on talking.

In a lucid dream, I'm free to try any number of techniques without real-world penalties. I made several different comments, some of which offended her and some of which had no effect at all. Eventually, I said, "Your insights involve a level of detail that's fascinating, but that falls outside the scope of this workshop. You might consider writing an article, posting it to your web site, or even writing a book on the subject. Now, to pick up where we left off . . ."

As a result of that dream interaction, I realized that what I said wasn't as important as how quickly I followed my interruption with a resumption of the class material. Later, in an actual workshop, I faced this exact situation ... and, because I had practiced in my lucid dream, I was able to interrupt gently and—bam!—segue right back into my material without hurting anyone's feelings or losing control of the presentation.

—*Mark, 41*

* * * * *

The last thing I wanted to do was ask my boss for a raise. Every time I thought of going into his office, I just became this inarticulate idiot. No matter how I tried to come up with something direct to say, I found myself making false starts and changing the subject.

I was so worried about the situation, I started dreaming about it. In my dream, though, I wasn't myself. Instead, I was very frank, very straightforward. "If I can't get a raise," I said, "I'll have to look elsewhere, even though I love my job here very much."

In the dream, my boss nodded and started asking questions. I decided to try the same approach at work the next day, and it worked.

—*Roger, 37*

Tips and Techniques

Power naps. I firmly believe my habit of generating vivid, highly detailed, and realistic rehearsals in my waking world helped me with lucid dreams in general ... and made it easier for me to create lucid practice sessions, in particular.

While I don't use this technique at night, I frequently study material just before taking a power nap in the afternoons. Occasionally, I even allow myself to drift off to sleep while reading and organizing course outlines.

I find that I easily carry the presentation over into a short dream, where I can present it and gauge its effect on the audience. And, of course, you can use this technique to practice the delivery of anything: courses, lectures, proposals, invitations, readings . . . anything at all. In the lucid state, if what you're doing isn't well received, you can always "reset" the audience and start over.

Take a Walk on Your Wild Side

It's just a fact: a lot of lucid dreamers I speak with enjoy the complete freedom of sexual expression they experience in lucid dreams. In the dreamworld, there are no rules and no limits. Norms can be set aside. Indulgences can be pursued without concern for disease, pregnancy, or infidelity.

* * * * *

Our family was very uptight about sex, and nobody really talked about it. Church gave us the impression that sex was dirty and wrong. Since pleasing my family was very important to me, I really was squeaky clean all through high school and into my college years and didn't do anything with anybody.

The downside of this was that in my dreams I wasn't having sex either. When someone approached me, I would say no, or make excuses, or do any of the things I do in the real world. That really made me mad, because here's the only place I can let loose, you know? And I'm not doing anything, because I keep saying, "It's wrong."

This went on for years. Then, when I was a junior in college, I had this dream about this incredible guy—my fantasy guy, I guess. He was really into me, and he kept making moves. Just as I was about to back away, it hit me: I was dreaming. I don't know what gave it away—I just knew it.

I thought I would wake up, but I didn't. So I rushed him, because I was afraid I would wake up.

After that, more and more often, I would have a sex dream and realize I was asleep, and found out I could do anything I wanted. I'm not sure, but I think it's helping me be less uptight in the daytime, too.

—Kevin, 34

* * * * *

My boyfriend and I decided to be celibate during our engagement. It's not easy, since we both like sex and used to be very active with each other. Now, when I realize I'm dreaming, I just wipe everything away, call him to me, and go for it. It relieves a lot of tension, and I wake up feeling great.

At first, Jay was jealous, because he doesn't lucid dream. Now, he jokes that he's afraid I'll decide Dream Jay is better than he is . . . and that I'll leave the real Jay for the one in my dreams!

—Katrina, 20

* * * * *

AIDS and syphilis and herpes and super-gonorrhea . . . I mean, what's next? And who needs it? I don't want a disease, and I don't want a baby right now, and I sure don't need the complication and drama of a partner when I'm just getting my own life back together.

In lucid dreams, I can relax in a way I could never relax in the real world. Whatever comes up, I can go for it. I've been a man. I've been a woman. I've been with men and women. I've been to orgies. If anyone invited me to an orgy in real life, I'd die twice of embarrassment.

> My dream lovers are gentle, good at what they do, and
> I don't have to fix anybody breakfast or worry about who's
> going to call who the next day.
>
> *Janice, 29*

Tips and Techniques

Dream tokens. A lucid dream gives you the opportunity to meet your fantasy lover. Many people, though, have very vague ideas about their dream lovers' identities. What would your dream lover look like? What would his or her personality be like? What kind of things would you do together?

A dream token—a collage, a list of your dream lover's perfect traits, a photograph of the actor you fantasize about, or even an item of clothing that he or she might wear—can be an effective way to focus your intentions. Keep the token near your bedside. Each night, before going to sleep, spend a few minutes contemplating the token and meditating on the kind of encounter you would like to have with your fantasy lover.

As you drift off to sleep, gently bring your thoughts back to your fantasy. Continuing this practice over several nights will not only increase your chances of encountering your lover in your dreams, but may also help you recognize him or her as a dream cue . . . and aid in your pursuit of lucidity, as well.

Dream meetings. Separated from a lover? Instead of the usual chat or phone sex, try arranging a tryst in the world of dreams.

Over a series of nights, "synchronize" yourselves by talking about and anticipating your meeting in the dreamworld.

Picture the setting in detail. Discuss what you'll do when you find each other there. During the day, whenever you think of your lover, pause for just sixty seconds and imagine a lucid dream in which the two of you can be together.

Later, watch for dream cues and opportunities to assume control of your dream state. Discussing and practicing your dream date in advance will make creating and experiencing it in the dreamworld much easier. Back in the waking world, you can compare notes with your partner.

To-do lists. During the day, instead of indulging in waking fantasies, tell yourself, "I'll do that in my next lucid dream." Immediately afterward, perform a reality check. Are you dreaming? Look for a headline, a book, a sign, or a clock, and confirm whether or not you're in the waking world.

As you make this a habit, you will eventually, in a dream, encounter a sexual situation. By reflex, you'll say, "I'll do that in my next lucid dream" and perform the reality check. When the dream cues alert you to the dream state, you'll become lucid and be free to pursue the fantasy you've been hoping to experience.

Chapter 8 in a Nutshell

As you begin to have lucid dreams more frequently, common pastimes—flying, world building—may become a bit passé. Fortunately, the applications of lucid dreaming are as variable and flexible as the dreamworld itself. With a little effort and creativity, you can utilize lucidity to explore alternative time lines and past lives; escape your physical body; communicate with friends and relatives, living or dead; contact your dream guides; perform interactive dream analysis; heal your physical or emotional scars; overcome fears and build confidence; and even revel in your wildest fantasies.

What's Next?

Having expanded the horizons of lucidity with these applications, now would be the perfect time to explore how to analyze the people, scenes, and symbols encountered in the dreamscape. Chapter 9 provides an approachable guide to dream analysis for both lucid and traditional dreams.

nine

Interpreting
Lucid Dreams

A Brief History of Dream Interpretation
The Dreams of the Ancients

Humanity has a long history of turning to dreams for insight and instruction. Included in Jean Bottero's *Mesopotamia: Writing, Reasoning, and the Gods* is an essay entitled "Oneiromancy," detailing the practice of Mesopotamian dream interpretation. Based on a study of ancient language, Bottero concludes the Mesopotamians understood the difference between the dreaming and conscious state, attributed the unusual vividness of dreams to the god that originated them, and scoured their dreams for hidden meanings.[1]

---

1 Jean Bottero, "Oneiromancy," in *Mesopotamia: Writing, Reasoning, and the Gods*, trans. Zainab Bahrani and Mark Van De Meiroop (Chicago: University of Chicago Press, 1995), 108–110.

The Egyptians believed dreams contained important messages. Troubled individuals would sleep in temples, then request dream interpretations from priests. Egyptians frequently interpreted dreams using an elaborate system based on puns.[2] The word for "great," for example, sounded a great deal like the word for "donkey"; as a result, dreams of donkeys were considered harbingers of extremely good luck.[3]

An ancient Egyptian book of dream interpretation, the *Dream Book*, contains a catalog of more than 100 dreams. The logic behind the interpretation is not revealed, but the prescriptions are precise and deliberate: dreaming of eating crocodile meat, for example, was believed to indicate success in upcoming elections.[4]

The ancient Greeks borrowed the practice of seeking dream revelations by sleeping in temples, often sleeping in a specific temple for weeks or months in an effort to dream a particular dream. Early Greek poets, including Homer, positioned dreams as messages from the gods, but later philosophers dismissed this idea, preferring, as Aristotle did, to emphasize the symbolic nature of dreams. With an eye toward dream interpretation, Aristotle concluded that "the most skillful interpreter of dreams is he who has the fac-

---

2 Nancy Joseph, ed., "Why Freud Should Credit Mesopotamia," *A&S Perspectives,* Winter/Spring 2002, http://www.artsci.washington.edu/news/WinterSpring02/Noegel.htm (accessed April 20, 2006).

3 Anita Stratos, "Perchance to Dream," *Tour Egypt!,* http://www.touregypt.net/featurestories/dream.htm (accessed April 20, 2006).

4 Ibid.

ulty of absorbing resemblances . . . dream presentations are analogous to the forms reflected in water."

Artemidorus, who lived in the second century BCE, wrote a lengthy tome on the interpretation of dreams, based on interviews he conducted with large numbers of dreamers. In his book, he provides specific meaning for specific symbols ("A serpent signifies a king because of its strength . . . the crocodile signifies a pirate, a murderer, or a man who is no less wicked") and frankly discusses the meaning of sexual dreams ("The penis corresponds to one's parents . . . [and is also] a sign of wealth and possessions because it expands and contracts").

Dream Interpretation in Biblical Times

Throughout the book of Genesis, the Hebrew God uses dreams to communicate with everyone from Abimelech to Abraham. In the story of Joseph, Jacob's favorite son enjoyed a series of dreams indicating he would rise above his mundane life on the family farm and ascend to world leadership. His brothers didn't need to consult a dream dictionary to interpret the meaning of all those bowing sheaves of corn and stars. In the end, daunted by Joseph's potential, they faked his death and sold him into slavery.

Later, Joseph's ability to interpret dreams played a primary role in launching him from the prison to the palace. When dreams of cannibalistic cows kept Pharaoh tossing and turning, Joseph converted the king's bizarre visions into an accurate forecast of the upcoming famine. His interpretive skills scored him the number two position, leaving him second only to Pharaoh himself.

King Nebuchadnezzar's dreams were so disturbing he pushed them out of his memory. When he challenged his magicians and advisors to interpret the dreams he repressed, they balked, claiming symbols were needed to access the meaning of a dream. Daniel, a Hebrew prophet, was able to help the king by retrieving and interpreting the forgotten images.

The first few pages of the New Testament's Gospel of Matthew are rife with dreams. When God appears to Joseph and instructs him to overlook Mary's pregnancy, God does so in a dream. The scholars from the East (astrologers, most likely) are warned by God in a dream not to reveal to King Herod the location of the infant Christ. Later, God uses dreams to alert Joseph to Herod's death.

Pilate's wife begged him to have nothing to do with the crucifixion of Jesus, noting "I have suffered many things this day in a dream because of him."

Even the Christian practice of receiving the Holy Spirit, literally "the breath of God," is accompanied by the reception of meaningful dreams. "I will pour out my Spirit upon all flesh," God says, in the Book of Acts, Chapter 2. "Your sons and your daughters shall prophesy, and your old men shall dream dreams."

Modern Psychological Dream Interpretation

Perhaps taking a cue from Aristotle, who asserted the symbolic nature of dreams, modern psychologists and psychiatrists continue to examine dreams for insight into the mental and emotional health of their patients. In his masterwork *The Interpretation of Dreams*, Sigmund Freud argued that dream symbols could be "followed backward from a pathological idea into the patient's memory."[5] After dividing a dream into fragments, Freud would engage patients in the extraction of meaning. These meanings were believed to be distorted or encoded, and supervised therapy was positioned as the primary tool for teasing them out.

Carl Jung suggested that dreams follow a four-act structure found in novels and plays. He taught that the initial act, or the "exposition" of a dream, contained a statement of the problem under consideration. With the setting and initial situation established, the second act of the dream would begin, in which some form of complication or challenge would be encountered. During the third act, or "culmination," the dreamer would respond to the challenge in some way. The fourth act (which Jung called the "lysis") concluded the dream and was believed to contain a possible solution for the dreamer's real-life crisis.

Unlike Freud, whose interpretative methods were authoritarian, Jung believed in a more organic, straightforward process. Patients were encouraged to consider personal, cultural, and mythical associations for each dream symbol. Finally, through the process of "active imagination," dreamers could free-associate their way to a valid interpretation of their dreams.

---

5 Sigmund Freud, "The Method of Interpretation," chapter 2 in *The Interpretation of Dreams*, http://www.psywww.com/books/interp/chap02.htm (accessed April 20, 2006).

Simple Dream Interpretation, Step by Step

The business of dream interpretation is no longer the exclusive domain of therapists and counselors. While trained professionals can provide invaluable insights and useful objective input, interpreting your own dreams is a healthy, straightforward practice. Anyone passionate enough about dreaming to pursue lucidity is likely well-positioned to interpret his or her dreams, lucid or otherwise!

The simplified method of dream interpretation presented here is based on models used by professional therapists and counselors. It is easy for beginners to explore with confidence, but complex enough (especially with a little tweaking!) to serve the needs of the most advanced lucid dreamer. With a little practice, you'll be able to apply the method without referring to the step-by-step process in this book.

Especially if you keep a dream journal, you will find the following method tremendously useful. Jung believed interpreting a series of dreams could provide greater insight than interpreting an isolated dream, simply because, over time, the dreamer would become aware of repeating themes and patterns. Using the process outlined here, the dream cues you've already identified will provide you with invaluable insights.

Step One: Record the Dream

If you already keep a dream journal, you've got a jump on Step One. As with a dream journal entry, the goal here is not to write the Great American Novel. Instead, record every detail you recall as quickly as possible.

Here's an example drawn from the dream journal of a friend of mine:

I was in London. I knew I was in London because of the fog, and I could see Big Ben. I could also smell the River Thames, which, in this dream, struck me as especially foul.

While crossing a bridge over the river, I looked down and saw that the water was packed with icebergs: sharp, white, glittering chunks. I was immediately concerned, because I believed that tourist boats would hit the icebergs and sink, just like the *Titanic* did.

I found a patrolman and warned him about the icebergs. He seemed unconcerned and suggested I concern myself with other things. Specifically, he said I should get a hot pretzel and relax.

Prefer to keep things as simple as possible? Record your dream as a simple list of symbols. Here's how the dream captured above would look if rendered as a straightforward series of dream elements:

- London

- Fog

- Big Ben

- River Thames

- Bridge

- Icebergs

- Tourist boats

- Patrolman

- Suggestion

- Pretzel

Step Two: Outline the Dream

Jung asserted that dreams, like plays and movies, can be broken down into four discreet acts, with each act corresponding to something you need to know. Here's how my friend's dream of London looks when organized into a four-act structure.

ACT I: Setup/Statement of Problem. I was in London. I knew I was in London because of the fog, and I could see Big Ben. I could also smell the River Thames, which, in this dream, struck me as especially foul.

ACT II: Complication or Challenge. While crossing a bridge over the river, I looked down and saw that the water was packed with icebergs: sharp, white, glittering chunks.

ACT III: Culmination/Response. I was immediately concerned, because I believed that tourist boats would hit the icebergs and sink, just like the *Titanic* did. I found a patrolman and warned him about the icebergs.

ACT IV: Conclusion/Possible Solution. [The patrolman] seemed unconcerned and suggested I concern myself with other things. Specifically, he said I should get a hot pretzel and relax.

If you prefer to work with a simple list, you can do the same thing:

ACT I: London, fog, Big Ben

ACT II: River Thames, bridge, icebergs

ACT III: Tourist boats, patrolman

ACT IV: Suggestion, pretzel

Step Three: Make Associations

Having outlined your dream, you can now begin the process of making associations between the elements of your dream and your own experience. When my friend tried the process, he came up with these ideas:

ACT I: Setup/Statement of Problem

- London: expensive to visit, far away, tea, the Queen, an empire, the Union Jack

- Fog: cold, clammy, spooky, ghostly

- Big Ben: time, tall, tower, bells

ACT II: Complication or Challenge

- River Thames: history, historic river, flowing, moving

- Bridge: going over, getting over, linking, connecting

- Icebergs: cold, frozen, dangerous, just the tip visible, floating

ACT III: Culmination/Response

- Tourist boats: frivolous, unnecessary, noisy, expensive

- Patrolman: authority, rules, regulations, enforcement

ACT IV: Conclusion/Possible Solution

- Suggestion: misunderstanding, wrong thinking, shift in perspective

- Pretzel: simple, inexpensive, flavorful, warm

Step Four: Analyze the Dream

With nothing but his outline and associations to guide him, my friend surprised himself with the following interpretation of his own dream:

> Based on what I can see here, the problem on my mind has to do with distance. For me, London represents an expensive, faraway place. Every element of my dream in Act I strikes me as heavy, troublesome, awkward. When I first looked at this list, I had no idea why these themes would be on my mind or what problem they might be connected with.
>
> When I look at the complication or challenge I'm facing in Act II, my associations are all about movement, connection, and danger. For some reason, thinking of the bridge as a challenge made me think of communication and the difficulties inherent in keeping in touch with someone far away.
>
> Right away, I thought of Mickey, a friend I haven't spoken to in years. We both agreed to make an effort to keep in touch after he got a new job in a city about three hours away. At first, we called and emailed each other all the time. Without meaning to, though, we've both lost contact with each other.
>
> I've been thinking of getting back in touch with him, but I've avoided it. After all this time, a simple email doesn't seem appropriate. I've been planning to call him, or go visit him, or do something bigger.
>
> And then, here comes Act III, which symbolizes my response to the problem. Look at my associations: frivolous, unnecessary, expensive solutions. And it's true: I'm perpetuating the problem of being out of touch by focusing on complicated, expensive solutions. Instead of just drop-

ping Mickey an email or sending him a text message, I've been waiting to find time to call or visit. At that rate, we'll never get together.

The patrolman's suggestion in Act IV is a great solution: go with something simple. Why complicate things? Just fire off an email, tell Mickey I've missed him, and break the silence. Nothing could be easier. He probably feels as bad about losing touch as I do.

I have to say: when I first wrote down this dream, I had no idea what it might mean. If anyone had told me that my dream meant this, I would probably have denied it. But after working it out for myself, I can feel the "rightness" of this solution. It works. And just yesterday, right before I had this dream, I came across an old email from Mickey and thought, "I need to get in touch with that guy," so having this dream, looking back at things, makes perfect sense.

Interpreting Lucid Dreams

Analyzing your dreams will lead you to a wealth of personal insight. Using this same process, you can also analyze your lucid dreams. By their nature, lucid dreams are more vivid, more realistic, and easier to recall. When you begin to analyze them, you may find that their symbolic messages are also more pointed, more revealing, and even more important than those of other dreams.

Below, you'll find three simple methods for interpreting lucid dreams. Since these methods will generate very different kinds of personal revelations, I encourage you to try them all.

Method One: Standard Analysis

With standard analysis, you treat your lucid dream exactly as you would any other. As an example, here's a lucid dream from the dream journal of Emilee, a thirty-eight-year-old single professional from Oregon:

ACT I: Setup/Statement of Problem. Because it was my birthday, I was expecting my mother to come for a visit. I was rushing around the apartment, cleaning up (she's picky about that sort of thing).

ACT II: Complication or Challenge. No matter how much I cleaned up, the apartment just looked worse and worse. When I tried to vacuum, for example, I damaged the carpet and water bubbled up into the apartment. By the time the doorbell rang, I was up to my knees in dirty water.

ACT III: Culmination/Response. At this point, I realized this was a dream. (I live in a second-floor apartment, and the idea of water bubbling up to the second floor from underneath the carpet struck me as suddenly impossible.) I got out of there fast. I pushed the apartment away and jumped up and down until I landed in my target space: an outcropping of rock along my favorite hiking trail.

ACT IV: Conclusion/Possible Solution. I felt so relieved, excited, and safe! The wildflowers along the trail were brighter than I'd ever seen, and the air was especially clean and cool. I managed to spend several minutes wandering the trail before I woke up.

With her outline completed, Emilee made associations for each of the major symbols in her dream:

ACT I: Setup/Statement of Problem
- Birthday: concern, getting older, still single, ignore it
- Mother's visit: stress, never happy, crazy-making
- Cleaning: hiding things, putting on a happy face when things aren't happy

ACT II: Complication or Challenge
- Effort makes things worse: happening a lot lately, at work, with boyfriend
- Damaged carpet: something that needs repair
- Flooding: bad situation getting worse, messy, smelly, escape it
- Doorbell: signal, alert, message telling you someone is there

ACT III: Culmination/Response
- Becoming lucid: time to wake up, assume control, take the wheel, be responsible
- Getting out: escape, moving on, getting away, removal, step back
- Hiking trail: peaceful, beautiful, isolated, quiet, distant

ACT IV: Conclusion/Possible Solution
- Feeling safe: a reminder I can feel safe, my mood is up to me
- Wildflowers: wild, break rules, out in the open, untended
- Cool air: refreshing, open, unrestricted, clean

When Emilee reviewed her list of associations, she laughed out loud.

> Okay, this isn't really subtle, is it? I'm trapped in a relationship with a guy, and I'm mostly with him because he drives my mother crazy. That really is the case, and I've been thinking about breaking it off, but I've been concerned about being alone and worried that, with pressure at work, I won't have time to meet anyone else. Every birthday is a reminder that meeting the right guy is getting harder and harder to do.
>
> And the Act II challenge is true, too: I know I need to fix this. I'm not happy, he's not happy, and the doorbell's been ringing for weeks. But I keep putting off making a decision and sticking to it. It's also meaningful for me that I became lucid and took control at the exact point when I became critical of the situation. In real life, I need to do the same thing: be critical and take control. It's time to step back from my situation and isolate myself.
>
> I want to feel as free and unrestricted as those wildflowers. I think the message of this dream is clear enough: it's time for some major changes. Now I just have to find the time and energy to make them.

Method Two: Analyzing the Lucid Experience Only

While some dreamers feel assuming control of a dream shatters the subconscious message embedded within it, most lucid dreamers I spoke with felt their lucid episodes contained messages of equal (or perhaps even greater) importance. After all, while traditional dreams are entirely passive, dreams in a lucid state are interactive. In a lucid dream, you're as close as any person will ever come to having a direct, face-to-face conversation with your own subconscious mind.

Tapping into the wisdom of that conversation may be as simple as choosing to analyze lucid episodes as though they, themselves, are stand-alone dreams. Lucid dreamers who use this approach record, but do not analyze, their non-lucid dreams, preferring to analyze only the symbols they encounter while in the lucid state. Consider this dream from the journal of Quinn, a videographer:

> *Pre-lucid dream.* I'm standing in a casino, watching people play blackjack. Everyone is very excited because one large man in a black suit is winning lots of money. The woman standing next to me keeps saying, "The house is really takin' a beatin' tonight!"
>
> I have my camera on my shoulder, taping the entire event. Suddenly, a casino manager yanks the power cord, pulling me backward. When I turn to him, I'm furious. He puts his hand over the lens and tells me that photography in the casino is not allowed.
>
> The woman standing next to me turns to us, like she's about to say something important. "The house is really takin' a beatin' tonight," she says. She nods and repeats herself. "The house is *really* takin' a beatin' tonight."
>
> *The lucid dream.* Each time she says the phrase, her face and gestures are identical—like a clip played back over and over. Nobody in real life ever looks like that. In fact, seeing something replayed over and over again has become one of my dream cues, so I know I'm dreaming.
>
> *ACT I: Setup/Statement of Problem.* I realize suddenly that I can use my camera like a fire hose, spraying out some kind of energy. I use this to sweep the unpleasant manager away. He sprawls head over heels, rolling back behind a craps table.

I feel like running, so I will the casino away and call up a stretch of highway I used to drive on in Arizona. In a lucid dream, I can run really, really fast, and my legs move so quickly, they look like that cartoon circle that's under the Road Runner in the old Warner Brothers cartoon. When I look down, I'm wearing nothing but running shorts, so I take off.

ACT II: Complication or Challenge. I'm able to run as fast as I like, but I'm aware that I'm not making any real progress. The road moves under me, but the landscape stays exactly the same. It's like I'm running on a treadmill. I want the full 3-D effect, though, so that everything will seem as real as possible.

ACT III: Culmination/Response. The harder I try to focus on making the landscape look real, the less control I feel over the dream in general. The sky gets hazy, and other details, like the stripes on the road, become indistinct. I suddenly feel more exhausted than exhilarated, so I stop, crouch down with my hands on my knees, and work on staying in the dream.

ACT IV: Conclusion/Possible Solution. Overhead, I can hear some kind of bird screeching. I'm not sure whether it's a vulture, eagle, or hawk, because all I can see is the black outline against the sun. It looks a little like stock footage, the sort of thing they cut to when actors in a television show point up at the sky. The minute I focus on this, the landscape around me flares to life. It's more real than reality. When I look at it now, I can't believe I ever had trouble controlling the dream.

From this outline, Quinn made a list of major symbols in the lucid portion of his dream and generated associations for each one:

ACT I: Setup/Statement of Problem

- Fire hose camera: the power of what I do, the energy I channel through my work

- Running: escape, recreation, relaxation, fitness

- Highway: peaceful place, I like the heat, way to get from there to here

- Wearing shorts only: freedom, having the right equipment, openness

ACT II: Complication or Challenge

- Making no progress: being stumped, not being able to move forward, work right now

- Treadmill highway: I hate this, because I love running outdoors, but hate treadmills

ACT III: Culmination/Response

- Hazy sky and fuzzy details: the need for clarity or focus, need to dig deeper

- Exhaustion: tiredness, out of breath, at the end of my rope

- Crouching: defensive posture, do this to keep from throwing up sometimes

ACT IV: Conclusion/Possible Solutions

- Circling bird: thoughts in the back of my head, uncertainties, doubts

- Stock footage: easy but not effective, cheap but not "right"

- Hyper-reality: what life should be like, thrills, feeling empowered

With only a few minutes of reflection, Quinn could easily find meaning in the lucid portion of his dream:

> I love what I do, but lately, I hate what I do. Work has always been my escape. I come in early and work late because I love shooting and editing. Now, I find myself goofing off and wasting time for the first time in my life. I've got all the right equipment and every opportunity to do something meaningful, but the company I'm working for is wasting my time and talent because they don't have enough for me to do.
>
> I've been beating my head against the wall trying to figure out what to do, so I just keep going through the motions, like someone running on a treadmill. There's no joy in it any more, and I really resent the fact that something as shallow as a paycheck is keeping me locked into this position.
>
> Everything's out of focus lately. I need to get back to what I love to do: producing video that makes people's jaws drop. Instead of doing that, I've been giving in and letting this place leech away my energy. My response so far has been to crouch down and "take it," because I've convinced myself I need the money.
>
> In the back of my mind, I've been thinking of leaving this company and moving back home to the West Coast. At first, I told myself that kind of circling back would be seen as defeat or being beaten down, but now I'm thinking that staying here is like that stock footage: adequate, but not what I'm really after. I want that feeling of living in hyper-reality. I want to feel really deeply committed to my work again.

Method Three: Analyzing Lucidity over Time

By analyzing recurring themes in non-lucid dreams, you can become aware of patterns and spot dream cues. Along the same lines, you can analyze themes, activities, and events that dominate your lucid dreams . . . and learn important things about yourself in the process.

Over the course of four months, James recorded eight lucid dreams. In those dreams, he noted the following recurring elements:

- Flying (3 times)
- Riding jet skis (3 times)
- Sex with a celebrity (2 times)

James then treated these recurring activities as symbols, making a list of them and forging associations for each:

- Flying: defying the rules, breaking laws, doing something other people can't
- Jet skis: dangerous, fast, thrilling, stunts, impossible stunts
- Celebrity sex: forbidden, not likely, fantasy, getting away with something

James noticed that his lucid activities had one theme in common: in the lucid state, he was drawn to activities he felt were too risky to pursue in real life. "I'd never skydive, even though I'm obsessed with flying. After seeing my cousin's accident on a jet ski, I still ride them, but I'd never do the kind of stunts I can do in a dream. And my girlfriend insists on monogamy, so even if I had a chance to be with some supermodel, I'd risk losing everything if I went through with it."

After analyzing the nature of his lucid adventures, James decided he was yearning to break free of what had become for him a very stable, very comfortable, but somewhat dull personal life. Without breaking rules or disrupting the parts of his life he valued (his relationship, his job), he decided to look for some exciting new activities with an acceptable level of risk. "I won't be bungee jumping anytime soon, but I may go downtown to that place that lets you skydive over a jet engine, just to expand my horizons."

Chapter 9 in a Nutshell

The ancients believed that dreams were messages from the gods, and efforts to pursue and analyze dreams were taken very seriously. In biblical accounts, dreams are often positioned as direct communication from God, allowing the dreamer to glimpse the future, be warned of impending disaster, or receive personal spiritual instruction.

Modern psychologists and psychiatrists may discount connections with deity, preferring to see dream symbols as windows into the subconscious mind. Approaches differ, but simple dream interpretation usually involves defining the dream story, extracting symbols from that story, associating these symbols with elements of the dreamer's life, and using this information to gain insight into the dreamer's state of mind.

Lucid dreams may be interpreted in much the same way. Dreamers may analyze the entire dream, or they may choose to focus only on the events and symbols encountered during the lucid state. By taking an objective look at what they choose to do when they can literally do anything, lucid dreamers learn a great deal about themselves and their deepest desires.

What's Next?

This book provides you with a comprehensive introduction to sleep, dreams, and lucid dreaming. You have in your hands everything you need to begin pursuing lucid dreams of your very own.

At a minimum, you should begin keeping a dream journal as a means of building dream awareness. (Need a refresher? See chapter 6.) This is the first tool most active dreamers employ—and likely the most essential. It will enhance your awareness of dreams in general and help you detect the repeating symbols and circumstances that will become useful dream cues.

As your interest in lucid dreaming grows, you may want to pursue the more scholarly books on the subject, including the works of America's foremost lucid dream researcher, Dr. Stephen LaBerge. His books, especially *Lucid Dreaming: A Concise Guide to Awakening in Your Dreams and in Your Life* and *Exploring the World of Lucid Dreaming*, are highly recommended for their firsthand accounts of Dr. LaBerge's research. You may also want to browse www.lucidity.com, the official web site of the Lucidity Institute. There you'll find opportunities to participate in the ongoing research conducted by the institute, along with products and services of special interest to lucid dreamers.

In your dreams, of course, the options and possibilities are endless. As you continue your own quest for lucidity, be sure to take the time to enjoy all the potential lucid dreams have to offer you, both in the waking world and in the dreamscape.

Sweet dreams!

Bibliography

The following works were consulted during the writing of this book and are invaluable resources for those interested in pursing a study of lucid dream literature.

Aristotle. *On Dreams*. The Internet Classics Archive. http://classics.mit.edu/Aristotle/dreams.html (accessed February 22, 2007).

Bottero, Jean. "Oneiromancy." In *Mesopotamia: Writing, Reasoning, and the Gods*. Translated by Zainab Bahrani and Mark Van De Meiroop. Chicago: University of Chicago Press, 1995.

Carroll, Robert Todd. *The Skeptic's Dictionary*. http://skepdic.com.

Coren, Stanley. "Sleep Deprivation, Psychosis and Mental Efficiency." *Psychiatric Times* 15, no. 3 (March 1998). http://www.psychiatrictimes.com/p980301b.html (accessed September 17, 2006).

"Dire Risk if You Sleep Less than Six Hours." *CNN.com.*, n.d. http://cnn.netscape.cnn.com/news/package.jsp?name=fte/sleepdiabetes/sleepdiabetes (accessed February 2, 2006).

Freud, Sigmund. "The Method of Interpretation." Chapter 2 in
    The Interpretation of Dreams. Translated by A. A. Brill. 1911.
    http://www.psywww.com/books/interp/chap02.htm
    (accessed April 20, 2006).

Green, Ceila. *Lucid Dreaming: The Paradox of Consciousness
    during Sleep.* New York: Routledge, 1994.

Hearne, K.M.T. "Lucid Dreams: An Electrophysiological and
    Psychological Study." PhD diss., University of Liverpool,
    1978.

Horgan, John. *Rational Mysticism.* New York: Mifflin Company,
    2003.

Joseph, Nancy, ed. "Why Freud Should Credit Mesopotamia."
    A&S Perspectives, Winter/Spring 2002. http://www.artsci
    .washington.edu/news/WinterSpring02/Noegel.htm
    (accessed April 20, 2006).

Kelsey, Morton T. *God, Dreams, and Revelation: A Christian
    Interpretation of Dreams.* Minneapolis: Augsburg Fortress,
    1991.

Kirchheimer, Sid. "Sleep Deprivation Hinders Thinking,
    Memory." *WebMD.com,* March 14, 2003. http://my.webmd
    .com/content/article/62/71591.htm (accessed February 2,
    2006).

LaBerge, Stephen. *Lucid Dreaming: The Power of Being Awake
    and Aware during Your Dreams.* New York: Ballentine Books,
    1990.

LaBerge, Stephen, and Howard Rheingold. *Exploring the World
    of Lucid Dreaming.* New York: Ballentine Books, 1990.

LaBerge, Stephen, and Jayne Gackenbach. "Power Trips:
    Controlling Your Dreams." *OMNI* 9.7 (April 1987), 1–4.

Man from Mars Productions. http://www.manfrommars.com/
    tripp.html (accessed July 20, 2005).

Mass, James B. *Power Sleep: The Revolutionary Program that Prepares Your Mind for Peak Performance.* New York: Villard, 1998.

Murphy, Dennis. "Family Battles Fatal Insomnia." *MSNBC.com,* January 14, 2005. http://www.msnbc.msn.com/id/6822468/ ?GT1=6190 (accessed July 2, 2005).

National Sleep Foundation. "Can't Sleep? Sleep Facts and Stats." http://www.sleepfoundation.org/hottopics/index.php?secid =9&id=34 (accessed April 20, 2006).

Peneny, DK. "Peter Tripp." *The History of Rock 'n Roll.* http:// www.history-of-rock.com/peter_tripp.htm (accessed September 17, 2006).

Pueschel, Matt. "Sleep shown as central to overall physical health." *U.S. Medicine,* July 2004. http://www.usmedicine .com/article.cfm?articleID=898&issueID=64 (accessed April 20, 2006).

Rechtschaffen, A., B. M. Bergmann, C. A. Everson, C. A. Kushida, and M. A. Gilliand. "Sleep Deprivation in the Rat." *Sleep* 25, no. 1 (February 1, 2002): 68–87.

"Sleepless in Gotham." *TIME.com,* February 9, 1959, http:// www.time.com/time/magazine/article/0,9171,892201,00 .html (accessed July 14, 2005).

St. Augustine. Letter 159, paragraphs 3 and 4. *NewAdvent.org.* http://www.newadvent.org/fathers/1102159.htm (accessed February 22, 2007).

Stratos, Anita. "Perchance to Dream." *Tour Egypt!* http://www .touregypt.net/featurestories/dream.htm (accessed April 20, 2006).

van Eeden, Frederik. "A Study of Dreams." *Proceedings of the Society for Psychical Research* 26 (1913). http://www.lucidity .com/vanEeden.html (accessed February 2, 2006).

To Write to the Author

If you wish to contact the author or would like more information about this book, please write to the author in care of Llewellyn Worldwide and we will forward your request. Both the author and publisher appreciate hearing from you and learning of your enjoyment of this book and how it has helped you. Llewellyn Worldwide cannot guarantee that every letter written to the author can be answered, but all will be forwarded. Please write to:

Mark McElroy
℅ Llewellyn Worldwide
2143 Wooddale Drive
Woodbury, MN 55125-2989

Please enclose a self-addressed stamped envelope for reply,
or $1.00 to cover costs. If outside U.S.A., enclose
international postal reply coupon.

Many of Llewellyn's authors have websites with additional information and resources. For more information, please visit our website at:

www.llewellyn.com